MW01658479

how to SELF-PUBLISH

A Guide for Author-Preneurs

2nd edition

by Kayla Fioravanti

Other Books by Kayla

Puffy & Blue: The Chronicles of Nine Lives Together

How to Make Melt & Pour Soap Base from Scratch: A Beginner's Guide to Melt & Pour Soap Base Manufacturing

DIY Kitchen Chemistry: Simple Homemade Bath & Body Projects

The Art, Science and Business of Aromatherapy: Your Guide for Personal Aromatherapy and Entrepreneurship

The Art & Science of Aromatherapy: Your Guide for Personal Aromatherapy

360 Degrees of Grief: Reflections of Hope

When I was Young I Flew the Sun as a Kite (Poetry)

Selah Press Publishing

How to Self-Publish: A Guide for Author-preneurs, 2nd Edition
By Kayla Fioravanti

2nd Edition Editor: Loral Robben Pepoon, CoWriterPro.com
1st Edition Crowdsourced Editing Team: Elin Criswell, Duane Bigoni, Patricia Di Gasbarro, Holly Port, Mary Humphrey, Rose Cunfer, Shila Nirola Laing, Cheri Perry, Petra Monaco, Alyssa Middleton, Carrie Petersen, Leigh Cronin, Pat Dunn, Debbie Richards, Kismet Andrews, Teresa Buchmann, Starla Ledbetter, Ron Carlson, La Shonda Tyree, Melissa Rivera, Robin Parker Schmidt, Maria Gelnett, Alana Rivera, Matt and April Leffingwell, Kim Jones, Jennifer Smith.

ISBN-13: 978-0692504413 (Selah Press)
ISBN-10: 062504419

Cover Design: Jennifer Smith, Eco-Office Gals
Printed in the United States of America, Published by Selah Press, LLC

Dedication

This book is dedicated to the reader, yes, you! To the person holding this book right now. It is dedicated to all the dreamers and storytellers who shared their dreams with me and to the ones I haven't met YET! This one is for you! Read it knowing that I wrote every word in hopes of inspiring you to spill your God-given talent out for the world to see.

TABLE OF CONTENTS

CHAPTER 1

•••

Becoming an Author-preneur

Roadmap

Technology is moving so fast, but the good news is that those changes will complement the information you are about to read about how to self-publish a book.

My intention is to offer you a road map with the understanding that "road" construction is constant, updating is imminent and improvements should be expected. I will update this book whenever major changes take place that would make the information on this map obsolete.

What is an Author-preneur?

Being an author in the self-publishing industry today is like opening a small business. Your books are your products. You must wear the hat of writer, editor (for early edits), publisher, publicist, social media manager and entrepreneur.

Being an author is a challenging career choice whether you go the traditional or self-publishing route. You expose your soul to the world and brace yourself for reviews.

If you decide to go the route of self-publishing, you give up the team behind the traditional publisher. You will need to do a lot of work yourself, hire people and ask for help. You will be your own cheerleader and give yourself a daily pep talk in the solitude necessary to write. It is the most rewarding gig ever, yet very tough.

Who Could and Should Self-Publish?

Over the past few years, the entire publishing world has been turned upside down. Who can self-publish a book? Absolutely anyone!

When I was younger, I dreamt of getting an agent and following the traditional route of publishing. Landing a writing contract with all its prestige was part of my dream. That was, until I had the opportunity in 2011 to listen to David Sanford speak about the publishing world at Multnomah University. It was then that the prospect of self-publishing wove its magic and the doors flung wide open for my new career path.

Throughout this book, I will break down what I learned that fruitful day and what I've learned through the process of self-publishing six books over the past four years.

Maybe the question isn't, "Who can self-publish" but instead, "Who should write a book?" My belief is that God gave each of us unique gifts and perspectives. Everyone has a voice and something important to teach. It is a matter of whether or not you have the confidence in yourself that what you know is worth sharing, and if you believe you are worth being paid for your gifts and talents.

> "If there's a book you really want to read but it hasn't been written yet, then you must write it." Toni Morrison

This commonly referenced quote is one of my favorites because it simply states the obvious. Write what you love, write from your heart and write what you are uniquely gifted to share.

I use the term author-preneur in this book because being both author and entrepreneur is critical to being a successful writer today. Self-publishing is the entrepreneurship route to publication. You are in control of deadlines, cover design, concept, price, as well as your potential success or failure. It's all yours, baby! You will see other terms commonly used for today's author including indie and artisan. I like all the terms because to me being an author-preneur, indie or artisan encompasses the innovative and risk-taking spirit it takes to succeed in today's ever changing marketplace.

> "Author-preneur: An author who creates a written product, participates in creating their own brand, and actively promotes that brand through a variety of outlets."
> Urban Dictionary

Whether you call this form of publishing indie, artisan or author-preneurship, the truth is that at the end of the day, readers don't care how your book was published. What they do care about is content, what it can do to help or inspire them, in addition to how much your book will cost them.

Once upon a time, self-publishing was equated with failure for an author, but it wasn't a true perception then and it most definitely isn't true today. It is just as exciting to hold a self-published book in your hand as it is to hold a traditionally published one. Maybe more so, because you get to keep a bigger piece of the profit; and you successfully accomplished your goal. My youngest daughter Caiden used to say, "I do it my own self" as she asserted her independence to the world. You can do it "your own self" too.

You are probably not going to get rich unless you are among the few one-in-a-million runaway success stories but in the meantime, why not create a long term source of income that will outlive you? Your royalty checks will continue rolling in forever. The book publishing industry is a multi-billion dollar industry. It is a risk to reach for the moon, but it's definitely more exciting than studying the lint in your belly button as you hold your dreams in.

Well-known and profitable authors are walking away from

traditional publishing to self-publish using On Demand Publishing for paperback editions, Digital options for eReaders such as Kindle, Nook and other devices.

In the book, *Be the Monkey,* co-author Barry Eisler discusses how he turned down a half million dollar book deal with a traditional publisher to self-publish. Not too long ago, he would have been considered crazy to walk away from such a deal, but he did the math. The decision to self-publish, just like any business decision, is a mathematical equation in which you commit to put your time, energy and resources into the most profitable route.

You don't have to look too far to find articles by established authors and publishers who look down upon self-published authors, but the ability to keep your book in print forever, earn higher royalties, achieve better eBook profits, set your own price and increase the speed that a book can enter the market, is swaying many over to self-publishing.

Joe Konrath, co-author of the book, *Be the Monkey,* puts it bluntly, "There are so many writers now defending the Big 6 (publishers) that I liken their behavior to Stockholm syndrome." Later in the same book Eisler says in regards to legacy deals, "The final argument I've been hearing . . . is that, 'Okay, some people are making money in self-publishing, but it's always the same names.' But the list of names keeps getting longer. The critics are going to be reduced to saying, 'Okay, some people are making money in self-publishing, but it's always the same five thousands names.' The critics will be self-publishing themselves before then."

There has never been a better time in history for you to write your book. The only things that stand between you and your published book are self-limiting fear, excuses or not making your dreams of writing and publishing your book a priority.

Using What You Already Have

If you are a business owner, have a blog, are a speaker, teacher, comedian, doctor, instructor, singer, preacher, social media maven, artist, photographer or otherwise already engaged in communicating with the public, then you've probably already written dozens of books-worth of material. You simply have not organized your thoughts, committed them to paper, or utilized channels of self-publishing to turn them into a book to create a long term (and low, one time effort) profit yet.

I'm here to tell you that you have a gaping hole in your pocket. Day in and day out, you are ignoring cash lying on the table that you could easily pick up and put to good use. By simply organizing your past efforts you can create future profits. Writing a book is not a get rich quick scheme in any way, shape or form. It is a method of sharing your knowledge with a larger audience and by doing so, profiting. If you are seeking to get rich quick then you are on the wrong path. If your life story will inspire others and your knowledge is empowering then by all means start typing, organizing, publishing and getting paid for your efforts.

Don't get tied up in knots wondering who would read your inspirations, jokes or life story since you aren't world famous yet. People won't care whether or not you are famous as long as your story is well written and is interesting. People enjoy reading interesting stories. Don't you?

You might think that people won't buy your book because you have already given the information away on your blog, teachings, hand-outs or a PDF. My experience has taught me that people prefer having all the information they want at their fingertips, rather than having to search all over the Internet to find it for free.

My book, *DIY Kitchen Chemistry,* is a collection of information I had already given away for free on YouTube videos titled Kitchen Chemistry, as well as on my blogs and website. I put on the cover, "As Seen on YouTube" and people still prefer to buy the book rather than watch videos or download and save all of the information.

Start with Your Dream

Not everyone has a treasure trove of old notes, teaching material and blogs to pull from to write a book. Many of you simply have a dream to turn your idea into a book. A dream is the first big step. Take the second step by harnessing the power of action. You might stand in the way of your dream, but if you are mentally and emotionally tough enough and if you can toss your excuses and fears aside, you are half way there. Nothing can stand in the way of your writing that book except you.

Sidetracked

Sometimes you may get sidetracked and lose your focus on the goal to write a book. Don't beat yourself up, just refocus and start again. If you fail along the way, it is okay to take a moment to have a pity party, but then let go and get on with the business of starting again. I will share universal writing tips that you can use regardless of your starting point in Chapter 3.

Stand Out in the Crowd

Authors face a new challenge today that wasn't present just a few years ago. The virtual bookstore is crowded! And I mean really crowded because self-publishing has removed the barriers to the publishing world and everyone can jump in. You need to stand out in the crowd. Your book should virtually pop and be full of good content that will send the reader back to buy more of your books.

Focus on your niche because that is what sells and brings people back for more. Out of my all of my books my best seller is, *How to Make Melt & Pour Soap Base from Scratch.* I was surprised because it is a very niche book. I expected it to drop off in sales, yet it continues to outsell my broader range books covering aromatherapy and DIY crafts.

What makes it stand out in the crowd of soap books to virtual strangers is that it teaches a form of soap making that none of the other books on the market teach. Most soap making books teach how to make handmade soap or how to use a bulk base called melt & pour soap. My book shares the previously well-kept industry secret recipe and techniques for making it from scratch.

Increasing Other Avenues of Sales

I wrote my first three books while we were in the process of selling our company, Essential Wholesale. I wanted to complete my handmade do-it-yourself craft, soap and aromatherapy books by the time the sale was completed.

These beauty industry books have provided a way for me to share what I learned and have continued income from the knowledge I accumulated while my husband and I owned Essential Wholesale. Because I self-published, I am able to keep my books in print long beyond my ownership in my brick and mortar business and even beyond my lifetime. With traditional methods, the publisher holds the power and decides when to print and when not to print.

Becoming an author gives you instant credibility and residual income. Having a book on the market increases your visibility to consumers way beyond your website and into popular online bookstores. Being an author opens additional doors for speaking. I received more speaking invitations after the publication of my books than any other time in the history of my business. Speaking is profitable, and it also allows you to interact with many more customers, without spending the money to fly to an event and pay for the event registration since as a speaker all your expenses are covered by the host.

I generally sell books to about 40–50% of the audience that I speak to at an event. Your sales numbers may vary depending on your audience, topic and book. When I spoke on the topic of my book, *How to Make Melt & Pour Soap Base from Scratch,* I sold out quickly.

Amazon Earning Avenues

Book sales are not the only potential way to earn income from booksellers like Amazon. You can become an Amazon Associate and earn an extra 4% or more of your own book sales and any other products that a customer buys on Amazon after coming over from your link. Bloggers can use your Amazon Associate account to link people to any other items Amazon sells when you write a blog post on any topic. For instance, if you write a recipe that has a funky ingredient, your reader will wonder where to buy it. Simply link them to Amazon from your blog post and profit. You may also choose to advertise for Amazon and earn even more extra income.

Amazon Associate Disclaimer: One of my editors took my advice after proofing this paragraph and discovered that Amazon would not approve her as an associate due to tax laws in her state. Before you start counting up your 4% earnings, be sure to go to the Amazon Associates program to determine if your state is included in the program. Also, this program could change if and when legislatures approve a national tax on online commerce.

CHAPTER 2

•••

A Comparison of Publishing Options

Self-publishing was never the route I planned on taking to fulfill my dream of becoming an author until I David Sanford gave a special talk to writers at Multnomah University. David Sanford is an author, editor, and the Director of Institutional Marketing and Special Representative of Corban University.

He started his talk by saying that traditional publishing is dead. Once he laid out his case, I dropped all aspirations to publish via traditional methods. David explained how Amazon's program ended the need for old school publishing as he walked us through the process.

Traditional Publishing

Because traditional publishing is costly, publishers have had to be extremely picky about selecting their authors. Tons of rejection letters have been received by authors who wrote amazing pieces of work including 60 rejection letters to Kathryn Sockett, author of *The Help*, 33 rejections to Mark Victor Hansen, author of *Chicken Soup for the Soul*, 23 rejection letters to Dr. Seuss, and many more. Eventually, these authors became well known. How many masterpieces sit in storage today, because self-publishing wasn't a viable option for them?

With traditional publishing, the publisher can take a book out of print at any time, leaving the author with no recourse or rights for future editions. This happens all the time in both the book and music industries. Recently, I spoke at an event that featured a famous author. I was in awe of just being in the same room, let alone on the same speaking docket! After the event, I stood in the lobby signing my books that the audience had purchased, while the other author stood nearby chatting with people. I later asked the other author why he didn't bring any books to sell, and his answer stunned me. Absolutely none of his books were currently in print which left him with nothing to bring to sell. What a huge loss for his pocketbook and what a disappointment for his fans who had hoped to buy a signed copy of his book.

If approached by a publisher with what seems like an amazing deal, you should consider it. Read all the fine print and know exactly what you are getting yourself into. Once you get a closer look at the numbers, ask yourself if they still have the same dazzle.

In, *Be the Monkey*, Barry Eisler and Joe Konrath broke down a typical $500,000 book deal into real numbers.

> $500,000 for a 3-year 2-book contract
> -$75,000 for your agent's cut
> $425,000 for a 3-year 2-book contract
>
> $425,000
> ÷ 3 years
> $141,666 per year

But what about taxes?

> $425,000 for a 3-year 2-book contract
> -$168,300 in Federal taxes equals (based on 2013 tax rate for $425,000 income bracket)
> $256,700 for a 3-year 2-book contract
>
> $256,700
> ÷ 3 years
> $85,566 per year

True, $85,566 per year for three years may be a decent income for some, but when you see that your $500,000 is reduced to $259,700 for a contract you are locked into for 3 years, you gain a better understanding. This also doesn't factor in state taxes. Your tax bracket may vary from person to person and year to year. Remember, I am an author and not an accountant, but I'm just simply pointing out the possibility of after tax revenue. Publishing, on the business side, is a numbers game.

After your advance, you will earn a royalty on every copy sold, but you first need to *earn out* the advance, so you won't see another check until you have sold enough copies to earn your advance at your royalty rate. If your book does not earn out your contract, then not another penny is earned and the book goes out of print. Thankfully, you don't have to pay the publisher back the money they advanced you. If your book does earn out your contract, you would make 10-17.5% royalty for as long as your book is in print and possibly an additional 25% on digital royalties if the publisher agrees to put your book into the digital marketplace.

A traditional publisher does have the advantage of experience and credibility. Traditional publishing is a hard place to get in the door, but you may end up there down the road. Some major hits were first self-published including: *Ulysses* by James Joyce, *The Adventures of Peter Rabbit* by Beatrix Potter, *What Color is Your Parachute* by Richard Nelson Bolles, *The Joy of Cooking* by Irma Rombauer and *A Time to Kill* by John Grisham.

Let me summarize a few highlights for you. Traditional publishers pay 10–17.5% of book proceeds, bring a book to market in 12–18 months and own the rights to your book. If you decide to go the traditional route of publishing, one of the things you will have to embrace is that it is slow paced. On the positive side (if you become one of the small number of current authors to experience it), there is a team of editors, marketers, graphic designers and sales folks supporting your efforts.

The negative is that one day, sooner than later; your whole team will walk away for a new author, leaving you in need to become an author-preneur to market your own book anyway. When traditional publishers walk away, they just might stop printing your book. If they put up an eBook version of your book, they will take a larger portion of your profits.

According to Joe Eisler, traditional publishers are paying 25% royalty on eBooks to authors and after everyone takes their cut, authors are actually earning as little as 14.9%. That might seem like a lot to you right now, but compare that percentage with Kindle Direct Publishing where an author gets a 70% royalty!

I promise I am going to show you how to put your book on Kindle and earn 70% royalty. The great thing is that your financial commitment to me ended with the price of this book. You get to keep the profits. After all, at the end of this self-publish race you will have earned it.

Vanity Publishing

Old school traditional self-publishing, once called vanity publishing, was a brutal and painful way to get your book into the marketplace. You had to spend tens of thousands of dollars up front and ended up with a garage full of books that you had to promote and sell out of your home. Publishing costs were a barrier that simply no longer exists. There are still some traditional self-publishing houses out there that charge the author an arm and a leg, but why go through unnecessary pain? Leave your garage space for your car, not your books collecting dust. On Demand books have rendered storing hundreds or thousands of self-published books an obsolete method of publishing.

PDF Style eBooks

The term eBook has two traditional meanings. One kind of eBook encompasses the PDF version of a book that is emailed to a buyers' inbox. The term is used interchangeably with the other version of eBooks that are bought online and go directly to a Kindle, Nook or other electronic devices. My comments below are in reference to the kind of eBook that is emailed in PDF format to the reader's inbox.

Publishing an eBook is an inexpensive method of bringing your book to market, but you can't control the profits from the book. Once someone has received a PDF copy in their email, they can forward a copy to anyone and everyone without ever paying the author. I have had several copies of books ranging from $0.99 to $150.00 sent unsolicited to my inbox for my opinion by such a customer. Once your eBook goes into the inbox of your customer you have lost control of it. Again and very important, it can be shared endlessly, without the author ever making another penny.

Note that Guy Kawasaki, a successful author, speaker and entrepreneur has a different opinion about eBooks, so before you rule them out based on my experience, I highly recommend reading his book, *APE, Author, Publisher, Entrepreneur.* Never limit yourself to one person's opinion when you are considering a business avenue.

In my opinion, the most negative aspect of a PDF style eBook is that your potential customers are limited to one's sphere of influence. Even if you have thousands of connections from social media, it is hard to imagine that your eBook, listed on your website, has more potential than it does on Amazon's website. Guy Kawasaki is a wildly successful author, social media guru and businessman who has the ability to sell his goods just as easily on his site as any other. Unless you share the same level of success and fame, eBook publishing on electronic devices is much more profitable and simpler than the PDF method.

On Demand Publishing

This method of publishing is low cost and easy to use. Your book prints on demand, which means the printer only prints a copy when the book is purchased so there is no stockpile of books for you to carry and sell on your own.

On Demand books yield high profits for the author and are available almost instantly online. There are countless companies that you can use to print On Demand books. I looked closely at all of them before I chose CreateSpace to publish my books. I have no regrets and the more I hear from people, who chose other companies, the more satisfied I am with my choice. For that reason, I am going teach you how to use CreateSpace to self-publish your books. CreateSpace is owned by Amazon, but makes your book available to other online bookstores in their expanded distribution. I will share some of the other major On Demand companies in this chapter.

When I attended David Sanford's talk, he mentioned Lulu and some other On Demand companies; however he said that CreateSpace was, in his opinion, the best one available. Taking my own advice, I did thorough research before making my business decision and agree that CreateSpace is the best option for author-preneurs.

CreateSpace sets a minimum price that you can charge for your book. It provides a royalty calculator so you can see your potential royalty payments by using different sales channels including Amazon.com, the CreateSpace eStore, expanded distribution to other online bookstores and Amazon Europe. Once you approve your proof with CreateSpace, a pop-up window will notify you about how long it will take to populate Amazon with your book. In my experience, it has always occurred within a 24-hour period for soft cover books.

The Reasons I like CreateSpace

- Everything about it is easy. CreateSpace is constantly making improvements. For instance, in 2011 I had to upload my book in a PDF format into CreateSpace and now you can upload directly from a Word Document. Since most books aren't printed in a standard 8.5" x 11" size, CreateSpace has developed Word templates so even a novice can successfully format their own book. If you have a PC or Macintosh using Word is the recommended method to write your book.

- You can upload your work as a print-ready .pdf, .doc, .docx, or .rtf.
- All rights to your writing remain yours.
- You are always in control. You can upload the same book under multiple titles and ISBN numbers if you want to. You can make changes to the interior or exterior of your book at any time without paying additional fees. The book you are holding in your hands is an example of an updated and changed book. The cover is redesigned and the interior has been updated.
- CreateSpace automatically lists your book on Amazon.com
- CreateSpace provides you with your own eStore, which is an online sales detail page where they fulfill all orders and handle the customer service.
- For a one-time fee of $25 CreateSpace makes your book available to expanded distribution: online retailers, bookstores such as Barnes & Noble, and distributors such as Ingram and NACSCORP within the United States.
- CreateSpace prints your On Demand books internationally so customers all around the world can read your book.
- CreateSpace makes it easy to select your price by providing a free royalty calculator. You will be able to calculate your royalty from the sale of your book through different outlets based on your particular price. You can easily change the sale price in the calculator until you are satisfied with the projected royalty amount.
- You can change your price at any time.
- CreateSpace does not charge for making edits to your book, whether they are on the cover or inside the book.
- You can print a book with as few as 28 pages or as many as 480.
- You may choose to enable Digital Rights Management (DRM). Caution: once you make the choice, you cannot change it. Don't make the mistake of enabling. I did on some

of my books, but learned that most successful authors do not recommend it. DRM is software that attempts to limit piracy, but is not always successful, and can cause problems for honest customers.

- CreateSpace sends you monthly royalty checks. You may choose to have the payment direct deposited for no fee, or pay a small fee to receive a physical check. You can change your method of payment at any time.
- Drop-Shipping feature: You can order copies of your book in any quantity and have them drop shipped to another seller or yourself. If you want to order copies of your book, the pricing at CreateSpace per book is much better than the prices elsewhere. The low price per copy comes in handy when you want to offer signed copies, bring books to an event or send some out for review. Drop-shipping also gives you an excellent option to sell your books wholesale to businesses. The books arrive with a packing slip that does not include the price of the books or the cost of shipping.
- There are no minimum order requirements for books ordered directly from CreateSpace. You can order one copy or thousands.
- CreateSpace has a huge community available to their authors. This is a free service you can use to talk to other authors, ask questions and find resources and tips.
- You can use any, all or none of the CreateSpace à la carte services including; editorial, illustration, layout and cover design.
- CreateSpace will provide you with the option of a free CreateSpace-Assigned ISBN, Custom ISBN, Custom Universal ISBN or allow you to use your own existing ISBN number. Every published book must have an ISBN, which stands for International Standard Book Number. All bookstores, retailers and libraries identify books by their ISBN number.

- CreateSpace prints an ISBN barcode on the lower back right corner of every book they manufacture.

Kindle Direct Publishing (KDP)

- The great thing about using CreateSpace is that once you have finished your process with them, they provide you with your book cover and interior files ready to quickly publish your book with Kindle Direct Publishing (KDP). In most cases you are simply a click, review and approval way from going live on Kindle. If you have heavy formatting, tables or pictures you might need to spend some time reformatting for Kindle.
- Kindle pays 35% or 70% royalty depending on which program you choose based on your book's sales price. It typically takes 48 hours to get your book to market.

COMPARISON OF ROUTES TO PUBLICATION

	Traditional	**Vanity**	**PDF eBooks**	**On Demand**	**Kindle**
Acceptance	Required	None	None	None	None
Costs	Publisher	$4000-15,000	Minimal	Minimal	Minimal
Time to Market	12-18 months	Varies	Immediate	24-48 hours	48 hours
Royalty	10-17.5%	100%	100%	35-70%	35-70%
Inventory	Publisher	100-5000	None	None	None
Advance	Yes	No	No	No	No
Copyright	Publisher	Author	Author	Author	Author
On Market	Months to Years	Forever	Forever	Forever	Forever

Intermediary Publishers

The following publishing companies are one stop shopping sources for copy editing, cover design, layout, formatting, marketing and so forth. I found it alarming that a number of the publishers on my original list of publishers I researched in 2011 were now closed, referred to a new website that didn't work or redirected me to an entirely new company. I feel confident recommending CreateSpace, which is owned by Amazon. The list of intermediary publishers below is current as of July 2015, but pricing and costs may vary with time.

Lulu

Lulu is a source for publishing books, photo books, calendars, eBooks and iPad Publishing. You can pick a package of services or buy their services à la carte. You keep your copyright and set your price. All payments from eBook retailers are made directly to Lulu and then paid out to you after taking a 10% cut out of your royalties. Lulu's minimum page count is 68 and maximum is 740 pages. Lulu offers à la carte services including cover design and illustration, editing, eBook publishing, publicity services, book reviews, promotional services, book fairs and books to movie screen.

Outskirts Press

Outskirts Press offers distribution, online listings, marketing support and order fulfillment. They offer additional à la carte services for professional copy editing, cover design, custom full color illustrations, private label ISBN, ghostwriting services and search optimization. They also sell kits for memoir writing, cookbook formatting, poetry formatting and fully illustrated custom children's books.

Blurb

Blurb specializes in photo books, yearbooks, cookbooks, wedding books, portfolios and more. Blurb's full color finished books are very expensive. For instance, a 20 page book can cost the author $12.99 to $50.99. In contrast, you can get a 300-page, full-color book with CreateSpace for under $40.

Virtual Bookworm

Virtual Bookworm offers full distribution, marketing, web design, book cover and interior layout and more for a fee. Virtual Bookworm was established as a "clearinghouse" for authors by a writer that was frustrated with traditional publishing. They review each manuscript and only offer contracts to authors whom they believe have exceptional manuscripts. You must submit your book for publication and then wait to hear if they accept your work.

BookBaby

BookBaby charges an up-front fee, but pays you 100% of your royalties. The fee structure varies depending on how many services you want BookBaby to provide. BookBaby distributes to Kindle, iPad, Nook, Sony Reader and more. The major drawback of using BookBaby is that they charge a fee for changes to your eBook. Also, you can change the price of your book one time per year with BookBaby without incurring a cost, but pay $50 per price-change if you do it more than once.

Author Solutions

Author Solutions is owned by Penguin Group (a traditional publishing company) and includes the brands AuthorHouse, Dellarte Press, Trafford, Xlibris, Palibro and iUniverse. Each brand has a separate website selling editing, design, printing and marketing services for your book. AuthorHouse retains ownership of your ISBN, cover and formatted files. This means that if you want to leave AuthorHouse, you either need to recreate your formatted book and cover and buy a new ISBN or buy them from AuthorHouse.

Update: In April 2013 and March 23, 2015, two class action lawsuits were filed against Author Solutions, Inc. Please investigate current status of the lawsuits for the most up-to-date information.

Selah Press

Selah Press is a one-stop-shop for book publishing, author coaching, platform building, business coaching and author services. Selah Press services and coaching helps you break down the mountains that have previously held you back into easy-to-manage ant hills. Selah Press takes NO royalties and charges NO ongoing fees. You retain the copyright, royalties and control of your book.

Other Devices

CreateSpace and Kindle Direct Publishing (KDP) are the first avenues for revenue I would suggest. After using these two amazing tools, it may be time for you to prepare your book for iBookstore, Barnes & Nobles' device the Nook, Kobo and Google Play. If you choose to participate in the KDP Select program when you publish your book via Kindle Direct Publishing, then you will need to commit to making the digital format of that book available through KDP for a 90-day period. You won't be able to distribute your book digitally anywhere else.

Since there are some formatting issues that need to be addressed to prepare your book for the other avenues, it is worth scheduling that project during your 90 days after KDP publication date.

If you don't choose to participate in KDP direct, you can start the process right away.

- iBookstore royalties are 70%.
- Nook from Barnes & Noble pays royalties of 40% or 65%, depending on the price point of your book.
- Kobo pays a royalty of 45% or 70% depending on the price of your book.
- Google Play pays a royalty of 48%.

The effort to prepare your book into the required format for each company might be well worth your time. Even though Amazon is the biggest game in town, it is important to weigh your options.

In 2014 I published *360 Degrees of Grief* on Kindle and Nook. During the time that I sold over a thousand copies on Kindle I had only moved one copy on Nook. I disabled Nook and went back to participating in the KDP Select program.

Smashwords

You can take a shortcut to create, publish and distribute your eBooks to Barnes & Noble, Kobo, eBookstore, Smashwords, Aldiko, Diesel eBook Store, Sony Reader Store, $tanza and more by using Smashwords. Smashwords takes a 15% commission of any revenue generated by your book. If an affiliate link generates a sale, then Smashwords takes a 29.5% cut.

It is an option to consider if you looked at the list of other online retailers and wanted to cry. Smashwords allows you to work only once to prepare your document in Word and then they do all the rest. The main drawback is that Smashwords does not review your files like KDP does. What you trusted them to do correctly for you is out of your hands and will be available to customers without your final approval on the formatting.

The Espresso Book Machine

The Espresso Book Machine is the newest gadget (at this time) to hit the book publishing marketplace that can print and bind your soft cover book in 10 minutes at the point of sale. I liken it to a book vending machine inside brick and mortar bookstores. It has quickly expanded with the addition of HarperCollins Christian Publishing and Penguin Group joining their network in 2013.

It can be used by authors to print drafts for a realistic view prior to having a proof ready, or to publish a book that you didn't write primarily for retail sale. The average price for an Espresso Book Machine finished book is $10-$15, (which is a lot compared to $2-$6 proof price from CreateSpace, but it is instant). I don't recommend going this direction yet, but keep your eye on this company in the future.

In 2015, On Demand Books and the Espresso Book Machine launched SelfEspress with writing, design, printing and distribution options. You can find out more at selfespress.com.

Amazon Imprint Publishing

Recently Amazon created a hybrid between traditional publishing and self-publishing. It basically takes all the good parts of traditional publishing like a book advance, editing, marketing muscle and merges them with the good parts of self-publishing including fair digital royalties, creative control and speed to market. The new dream for self-published authors is to be discovered for a deal by one of Amazon's Imprints rather than signing a traditional contract.

Amazon currently has AmazonEncore, AmazonCrossing, Amazon Children's Publishing, Montlake Romance, Thomas & Mercer and 47North. Recent announcements from Amazon include that they have acquired Avalon Books.

Barry Eisler recently accepted a contract with Amazon's Thomas & Mercer. This makes him an author with one toe in old school traditional books with his previous deals, one toe in self-publishing with continued projects and one toe into the new world of Amazon's Imprints. Regarding his deal Eisler said, "Publishing is a business for me, not an idealogy. . ." Like I have previously said, business is a math equation. You should keep all avenues open.

I have provided the Amazon Imprints website in Appendix 1 of this book for proposal submissions and inquiries.

CHAPTER 3

Advice from One Writer to Another

> "You must write every single day of your life . . . You must lurk in libraries and climb the stacks like ladders to sniff books like perfumes and wear books like hats upon your crazy heads . . . may you be in love every day for the next 20,000 days. And out of that love, remake a world." Ray Bradbury

In April 2011, after months of delays, I finally sat down to write my first book, *How to Make Melt & Pour Soap from Scratch.* My goal was to have the book written and published in time for a speaking engagement. My plan had been to start the book in January with what appeared to be just enough time to have it ready in May, and then life threw me a curve ball.

In January, my mother became ill, and in February, she died. My focus during those 3 weeks was on her care and comfort. I returned home to piles of work in my business and home. Around the end of March, I was mostly caught up at work, I sat down to write and I couldn't. Suddenly writing was more difficult than ever. Writing had always been directly connected to my heart. With the loss of my mother suddenly the flow was blocked and it was difficult to open the dam.

I was experiencing a major set-back. On one hand I had a goal. On the other hand I had a thousand and one excuses to not reach that goal. Under normal circumstances it seemed nearly impossible to write, edit and print a book in time for my speaking engagement. Now I was suffering with a serious case of writer's block.

I sat in front of my blank screen and had to choose whether I was going to embrace my excuses or my goal. I decided to reach for my goal. I started to write, realizing it might turn out to be half the book I planned, but knowing the right thing for me was to reach towards the goal no matter the results.

First, to get things flowing I organized and wrote all the technical stuff. I wrote for two weeks solid while conducting home-based experiments in my kitchen to make sure all the lab work translated to the kitchen chemist. After two weeks of writing the book was already more than I had planned from the beginning. I calculated if editing took one week to complete I would make it just in time. Editing took two weeks and the book grew. I figured I would make it by the skin of my teeth if layout, design and proofs took a few days. Those changes took another two weeks.

It would be an all-out miracle if the book printed by May; but then again, I believe in miracles! When the final proof arrived, I was on an overnight field trip with my daughters' school on the Oregon Coast. My husband Dennis acted as my eyes and reviewed the final proof for me. While walking through the woods with 5th and 6th graders, I talked Dennis through the final steps of accepting the proof and setting the ball in motion in order to get printed books to my speaking engagement in time.

I was scheduled to speak on May 18th and my books arrived at the speaking venue on May 17th. Miracles do happen!

Nothing, and I mean nothing, went according to plan in 2011. It seemed impossible to write, edit, layout and proof the book I had envisioned in time for the conference. And yet, it all came together.

I'm sharing the back story of my first book to encourage you that even when things don't go according to plan, aim for your dreams anyway. Embrace your goals, instead of the mountainous list of excuses that life presents. The conference date was going to arrive whether I tried to reach my goal or not. I was so thankful to have arrived at my speaking engagement with my goal accomplished, rather than kicking myself for not trying. I thought of the Will Rogers quote when I imagined arriving empty handed, "Even if you're on the right track, you will still get run over if all you do is sit there." I went on to write, edit and publish two more books by the end of 2011.

My Top Ten Tips for Writing a Book

1. Read

> "If you want to be a writer you must do two things above all others: read a lot and write a lot." Stephen King

A writer can never ever read too much. Read about writing, read successful authors in the genre in which you want to publish, read the cereal box, read fiction, nonfiction, magazines, blogs and fluff—just read. Reading stimulates creativity and inspires.

You can identify the books in my library that inspire me by opening the cover of the book and looking for my scribbling. A good book will have sections underlined and marked up. A great book will have inspired notes scrawled in the margins. When I'm stuck, I can get unstuck by flipping through the pages of one of the great books from my library and re-visiting my notes.

Read books on the topic you want to write on. Doing so will help you verify that you have something new and unique to add to the mix. You can also learn how successful authors have accomplished their goals and use their stories to inspire you.

While writing this book I read three current books on self-publishing including: *APE: Author, Publisher, Entrepreneur—How to Publish a Book* by Guy Kawasaki and Shawn Welch; *Be the Monkey —EBooks and Self-Publishing: A Dialog Between Authors Barry Eisler and Joe Konrath*; and *Dan Polynter's Self-Publishing Manual, Volume 2: How to Write, Print and Sell Your Own Book.*

My goal was to insure that I wasn't writing a book that had already been written. What I discovered was every author has their own unique perspective based on their experience. That unique perspective and writing style impacts readers based on shared life experiences. Having read all their books, I was able to see the value of a women's voice from the perspective of having started a successful business on a shoestring budget. There is a theme in the story of your life, your business and experiences that will connect with someone who has lived a seemingly parallel story line; those are the stories that need to be told!

2. Write

> "If I waited for perfection, I would never write a word." Margaret Atwood

Just write. I know that sounds trite, but it's true. Write junk for a few paragraphs if you have to, but get started. You can waste a lot of time and energy getting ready to start. When writing, don't edit as you go.

I was once in a writers group with someone who refused to use the words, "I" or "me" in his writings. This made for some awkward sentences and stories that got lost in translation. I could see the start of a great story and then it seemed like he lost track of what he was trying to say. Finally, I gave him an assignment to write without hitting the back space or delete buttons. He simply had to write and keep writing no matter what mistakes he made. He arrived with the most touching, heartfelt story he had ever written. Sure, it had grammatical errors, but it was beautiful and from the heart. Simply write. Editing is a separate process.

I'm a huge believer in the zero draft. A zero draft is the one no one sees. You should write your zero draft as if you are vomiting everything out onto the page. It should be full of mistakes and random ponderings. Get it all out on paper and then come back to it to cut, edit and blush about your grammatical errors. The zero draft allows you to write with the sole purpose of finding out exactly what you have to say. When writing flows uninterrupted, you have the opportunity to discover uncensored brilliance.

When you are done writing, write some more. Then when you have nothing to say, keep typing. When you have writers block, read to take your focus off the block for a few moments then start writing. The secret to writing is . . . writing!

Until I became a mother at 25 years of age, I wrote every single day. I started writing when I was in 5th grade. Writing was the life line I used to cope. A pen, paper and quiet was all I needed to wrestle out the thoughts in my head. Each day when I was done writing I felt a little lighter. Then life changed, stole my quiet time and solitude and replaced it with the non-stop pace of motherhood. I no longer write every day, but I write consistently. I set aside time that is designated for me to write. You need to determine how much time you spend writing based on the stage of life you are in, but don't just think about writing, do it.

3. Guard Your Time

> "Being a poet is one of the unhealthier jobs – no regular hours, so many temptations!" Elizabeth Bishop

Little things are the greatest stumbling blocks to writers. Things like laundry, dishes, TV, kids, text messages, Facebook, Twitter and phone calls are high among the distractions that steal your time. If you are serious about writing, the only way to accomplish your goals is to turn off the distractions for a specified period of time.

I have three kids. In order to set myself up for success, I tried not to choose time periods that had a high potential of needing to be kid time. But sometimes the kids had needs that took precedence. On those days, I waited until everyone was in bed before trying to write.

During your writing time, turn off the TV and radio, sign out of social media outlets and email inboxes, leave the phone in another room, and shut out the distractions that are your Achilles heel.

4. Join a Writers Group

> "However great a man's natural talent may be, the art of writing cannot be learned all at once." Jean Jacques Rousseau

Writers need other writers. No one quite understands the inner workings of a writer better than another writer. Most importantly writers need accountability. I have heard countless writers say that they need an agent just to get started. In reality, you need a writers group to bounce your work off of long before you meet with an agent. The writer's group critique is vital to moving a story forward.

I found my writers group by trial and error. I wanted a group of Christian writers so I started one at my church, it morphed, grew, shrunk and changed over the years. I've been invited into other groups along the way as well. It seems like when you are a part of a writers group, other opportunities suddenly open up. Writers need writers, period. End of sentence. Now go find your group.

5. Educate Yourself

> "If we knew what it was we were doing, it would not be called research, would it?" Albert Einstein

As long as I have breath in me, I will be seeking further education. I've never looked back and regretted learning something new. That is why I ended up in David Sanford's seminar. That one seminar swung all the doors open to the publishing world for me and removed all of my self-imposed shackles.

Take writing classes at your local community college or university. I took fiction and poetry writing in college long ago, but learned so much when I decided to take a journalism class at Multnomah University in 2011. Go to a writer's conference or retreat. The options are endless.

6. Create a Plan

> "All the words I use in my stories can be found in the dictionary—it's just a matter of arranging them into the right sentences." Somerset Maugham

Set aside an hour or two to brainstorm your ideas for the first ten books you want to write. David Sanford gave the attendees of his seminar this assignment. I couldn't wait to go home and start my list. I spent an hour following his advice and now two years later I already have the first four books from that list on the market. Even if you think that you only have one book in you, take the time to do this assignment. Get very specific as you write this list.

- Potential book titles
- Theme of each book
- Audience for each book
- Why you are uniquely qualified to write each book
- Steps you need to take to write each book
- What material you already have to start any of the books

I had written 54,000 words of my memoir, entitled *Puffy & Blue* but I put is aside to write this book because I felt others wanted to learn about the process of writing, publishing and promoting. I had learned so much in my first four books, so this book you are holding bumped ahead of the other book in progress.

The need to write this book took hold of me in February 2013. During 2011 and 2012, I had helped several new authors publish their books and then had been interviewed by Donna Maria Coles Johnson, President of Indie Business Network, on the topic of self-publishing. During this time, I was involved in helping others to self-publish. I didn't give much thought to writing a book about it.

After I published my fourth book, *When I was Young I Flew the Sun Like a Kite*, David Sanford asked me on my Facebook page when I was going to write a book about self-publishing. My friend Donna Maria Coles Johnson kept nagging, "You need to write a book on self-publishing."

I was successfully ignoring both of them though that little voice inside kept asking, "Why are you resisting?" To be truthful, I already had written three "how to" books and it didn't sound fun to write another.

While on the 2013 Indie Mastermind Cruise learning how to grow my own business, I was inspired to write this book. As I sat in a session with other small business owners listening to La Shonda Tyree empower her audience to teach soap making classes as a way of using their skills to increase their revenue my thoughts started flowing around empowerment.

Inspiration is like a seed, and as I thought of how empowered these women would feel if they knew how easy it was to self-publish, that seed grew and bloomed in the span of 30 seconds. As an alternative to teaching classes and handing out Xerox copies of their instructions and recipes, some of these women might prefer to self-publish as another source of income. The thought of empowering business owners to use their gifts, talents and information was all the inspiration I needed. When I shared the idea with the group, I knew I had to write it because they validated that a book on self-publishing would fulfill a real need in their lives.

You never know when seeds of inspiration will plant themselves. Though creating a plan to write is necessary, you need to be flexible enough to alter that plan when inspiration hits. My original plan was to return to working on *Puffy & Blue* after I finished publishing this book. However, I was inspired by the experience of grieving the loss of my mother to write *360 Degrees of Grief* instead.

7. Set a Deadline

> "I love deadlines. I like the whooshing sound they make as they fly by."
> Douglas Adam

Now that you know what you want to write, set deadlines for yourself. Without a deadline, you will have no goal to shoot toward. With that said, forgive yourself when you miss a deadline, and reset the goal. Don't use missing your deadline as an excuse to give up. I've missed every deadline that I set for myself, but I just kept going until I crossed the finish line.

One of my crowdsourced editors, Debbie Richards, said that she remembers hearing me say during a speech I gave in 2009, "I've been asked why I haven't yet written a book. I tell them, because no one has given me a deadline yet." Thank God I finally set my own deadline, took control of my publishing career and stopped waiting for someone else to do it for me.

8. Keep Notes

> "The hardest part is believing in yourself at the notebook stage. It is like believing in dreams in the morning." Erica Jong

My world is littered with little scraps of paper, bulging notebooks and scribblings. Life is inspiring all day long, every day. Write down the thoughts, words, memories, songs and unfinished thoughts that whoosh past you every day. Hang onto them, collect them and turn to them when you sit down to write. These little notes and notebooks are the ammunition that will help you fight the battle against writer's block.

If you don't have paper handy, use the voice recorder on your phone, leave yourself a message on your home phone or otherwise record your ideas before they lose their impact.

9. Blog and Use Social Media

> "The best time to start promoting your book is three years before it comes out. Three years to build a reputation, build a permission asset, build a blog, build a following, build credibility and build the connections you'll need later."
> Seth Godin

Promoting your book and yourself as a writer does not start the day your book is published, but it no longer takes three years to build a platform either. Create a platform today for the books of your tomorrow. Direct the traffic you create on social media platforms like Twitter, Facebook, LinkedIn, Pinterest, and Google+ to your landing place, either your blog or website.

Grab up your name on every social media platform you can find, even if you aren't ready to use them yet. Reserve your name so that when you are ready you aren't fighting for it. When you have an idea, reserve the website for it. You should own the (dot) com of your name, the name of your publishing house and any catchy phrase that you just might run with some day.

Remember you are building an author platform that will be essential in directing your target audience to your current and future books.

10. Write a lot

> "If you write one story, it may be bad; if you write a hundred, you have the odds in your favor." Edgar Rice Burroughs

William Stafford is my favorite poet. He was incredibly prolific during his lifetime. I remember reading that he sat down to write every single day.

> "Every day I get up and look out the window, and something occurs to me. Something always occurs to me. And if it doesn't, I just lower my standards." William Stafford

I think of that some days when I want something brilliant to appear on the paper and my mind is blank. I just start writing and remember that it is okay to "lower my standards" sometimes for the sake of getting the words flowing.

My husband thinks I should specialize in one genre of books, but I have too many genres in my head to give up on them all. It is wise to specialize, but for me it would cause me to sit at the computer in a deadlock with writer's block.

I wrestled with this concept for a while, and then I heard Erik Metaxas speak one day. His books range from serious biographies like *Bonhoeffer*, Christian books like *Everything You Always Wanted to Know about God*, and children's books like *It's Time to Sleep, My Love*. This made me feel better about my sometimes schizophrenic writing plan.

Final word of advice:
At the end of the day, there are no hard and fast concrete rules for writing that work for everyone. So, keep reading to shop for more ideas and direction.

> "There are three rules for writing. Unfortunately, no one can agree what they are." Somerset Maugham

CHAPTER 4
Budgeting Money

Once upon a time you needed a big budget to self-publish a book. Print On Demand and devices like Kindles, Nooks and iPads have completely changed the face of publishing. The costs can be free if you do it all yourself and select the no cost options off the à la carte menu in CreateSpace. Although Guy Kawasaki recommends budgeting $4,200 in his book *APE: Author, Publisher, Entrepreneur,* but I have never spent that much on publishing any of my books.

My point is that you can spend nearly nothing or you can spend a bundle. It really depends on your sphere of influence, how good you are at talking people into lending you a hand, how tech savvy you are on your own and how much money you can put into your project without it becoming a financial burden. If at the end of this exercise, you find that it will cost you more than you have in disposable income, just hang on because I will give you some advice on crowdsource fundraising later in this chapter.

Publisher and Author Logo

While publishing my first book, I didn't realize that CreateSpace required a name for my publisher, until we were ready to upload my book interior. A logo is not required; however I recommend a logo for branding purposes. I'm telling you now so you can plan for it. You are going to be branding yourself as an author and possibly branding your publishing house too. You want to stay consistent with your brand imaging. Your author logo may be as simple as the font you use to write your name on your website or as complex as you want. Your publisher logo should be simple and clean. It will go inside the jacket of your book and on the spine of your book. If you decide to use the free CreateSpace ISBN number (explained below) you can skip this step altogether.

Publisher Logo Costs

1. Free if you can do it yourself or ask a friend or family member to do it.
2. Amateur or Moonlight Professional $25-$100.
3. Professional $250-$1500.
4. Crowdsouring using Elance or 99designs is a great option too.

If you choose to get a custom ISBN, you will become the publisher. You need to come up with a name for your publishing house. Take the time to put some thought into this decision because it will be branded with you forever. Don't make it your name or the name of your book.

You may even end up setting up a separate website for your publishing house, so make sure it is an available name on the web and/or isn't trademarked in a way that you would be breaking trademark laws. Go to the Trademark Electronic Search System (TESS) to see if someone else has already gotten a trademark on the name you are considering for your publishing house.

Website Design Costs

1. Free if you can do it yourself or ask a friend or family member to do it.
2. Amateur or Moonlight Professional will cost you between $200 and $1000.
3. Professional will cost you $1000 and up.
4. Crowdsourcing using Elance or 99designs is a great option too.

Many factors can affect the price of your web design including whether you set it up as a brochure, e-commerce or blog format. I recommend setting up a blog format so that you can constantly update, share and keep the content fresh.

Keep in mind that your website is your Main Street America storefront. If setting up a website is above your head, don't hesitate to spend a bit of money getting your branding right. Make sure you look at the portfolio of the person you hire beforehand.

Editing Costs

1. Free if you crowdsource it among your social media contacts, beg your friends and family, tap experts in your field, your writers group and your High School and College English teachers. Be creative.
2. Amateur editor about 0.003 per word, minimum of $100.
3. You can check CreateSpace, Kirkus and Selah Press for current prices.
4. Professional Editing Services generally cost $65 per hour with an average of 10 pages per hour. You can do the math based on how many pages your manuscript is.

Editing is one of the most important places to spend your resources. It will be the difference between a professional and amateur book. And, don't panic if the prices have changed when you start your project. Remember, change is inevitable.

ISBN Cost

1. Free if you use the CreateSpace Independent Publishing Platform.
2. $10 for a custom ISBN.
3. $99 for a Custom Universal ISBN.
4. $250 if you buy 10 from Bowker Identifier Services.

I recommend a custom ISBN, Custom Universal ISBN or buying 10 ISBN numbers from Bowkers. The only positive side of having a

CreateSpace Independent Publishing Platform ISBN is that your book will be available to libraries and academic institutions through CreateSpace.

Remember ISBN stands for International Standard Book Number and is required for all published books.

Cover Design Costs

1. Free if you use the CreateSpace Cover Creator or are tech savvy enough to design your own to upload as a PDF using the specifications from CreateSpace. Be creative when you make your cover. You can use graphics or a photograph.
2. Starting at $399 you can have CreateSpace design a Professional Cover.
3. Graphic designers can charge anywhere from $250 to $1000 for a finished cover.

Layout Costs

1. Free if you either download the CreateSpace blank Word Template based on the dimensions of your book or if you are Word savvy and can create your own template.
2. Starting at $250 if you use the Professional Design Services at CreateSpace or Selah Press.
3. Or whatever deal you can work out with someone who will pay close attention to detail and set it up for you.

Proofing Costs

The cost of the printed book plus shipping. On average, your book cost from CreateSpace will range from $2 up to $5 each for a black and white interior book. I normally am so excited that I pay for the overnight or faster delivery choices. Every time you order your books from CreateSpace they will quote the price and estimated delivery date so you can choose the delivery method that fits your time frame.

Copyright Costs

1. Free if you don't register because all published AND unpublished works are automatically copyrighted. This topic is covered in more depth in Chapter 8.
2. $35 for online registration.
3. $65 for a paper filing.

Kindle Direct Publishing Formatting Costs

1. Free if you do it yourself.
2. Starting at $69 with KDP.
3. Starting at $250 with Selah Press.

Formatting for Other Devices Costs

The following options are ways to get your book into the hands of other eBook devices. It is not mandatory that you do this to sell books, but it is another avenue you can use.

If the following sounds too complex or expensive, you can always go the route of using Smashbooks and accepting a slightly lower royalty payment. Once you have one EPUB document created, all of the other devices accept files with the extension .epub. Only Kindle Direct does not use EPUB.

iBookstore Formatting Costs into EPUB

1. Free to convert it to EPUB and put into iBookstore yourself using the eBook software called Calibre.
2. $25.00 per hour if you email list@smashwords.com and request Mark's List of low cost formatters who will format it for you.
3. $29.99 per month if you subscribe to Adobe InDesign or $700 to buy InDesign to convert to EPUB.

Nook Formatting Cost for PubIt

1. Free if you choose to upload a Word document through Nook and format it yourself.

2. Free if you use the EPUB document you created for iBookstore.

Google Play Formatting Costs

1. Free if you use the EPUB document you created for iBookstore.
2. Free if you use a PDF version.
3. Cost of a book and shipping if you send a hard copy to Google for them to scan it.

Kobo Formatting Costs

Free if you submit book in your already formatted Word, MOBI or EPUB file.

Crowdsourcing Funding

If you just read through the above list with fear and trepidation about your ability to do some of the steps yourself and cannot financially afford to pay someone to do many of these steps, you should consider crowdsourcing for funding. The Internet has made asking for money to fund your big idea easier than it has ever been. You can ask friends, friends of friends, family and friends of family, as well as complete strangers, for their assistance. You can use a variety of different platforms to create a fundraising campaign that can spread like wildfire through social media. After doing my research and having seen several campaigns, I would choose Kickstarter if I needed to raise funds for my project.

Kickstarter

Kickstarter is a platform that specializes in helping you find funding for creative projects. You are in control of creating the campaign using pages, video and rewards for various funding levels. You set a deadline and funding goal for your project. People can make pledges towards your goal, but are not charged unless you meet your goal within the deadline.

It is wise to make your goal reasonable because a Kickstarter campaign is all-or-nothing. According to Kickstarter, currently 44% of projects have reached their goal on time. If your project is successfully funded, Kickstarter will charge a 5% fee of the funds collected.

Indiegogo

Indiegogo is an international platform that can be used to raise funds for any type of project. You don't owe any money until the campaign is successful. Indiegogo claims that you will gain global exposure from their one-click social media tools. This claim makes them unique.

On this platform you may choose to keep all the money you raise, even if you don't reach your goal with Flexible Funding or opt for Fixed Funding, which means you only get the money if you reach your goal. With Fixed Funding, you will be charged 4% of your goal if and when you reach your goal. With Flexible Funding, you will pay a 9% fee of the money you have collected. The danger of choosing Flexible Funding is that your contributors will be expecting a finished product that looks as good as it would have been had you reached your goal.

Unbound

Unbound specializes in funding authors. Unbound becomes both the fundraising platform and the publisher. Unbound splits the net profits of the book fifty-fifty with the author. If you support an Unbound author, your reward is your name printed in the back of the book and a limited edition copy of the book sent from Unbound. As you continue reading in this book, you will find that authors have the potential of making a much larger profit than fifty percent when they act as their own publisher.

Pubslush

Pubslush is another platform that specializes in funding for authors only. Pubslush allows for Flexible Funding and allows you to keep the money you have raised, even if you don't reach your goal. Pubslush charges 4% plus a 3rd party processing fee of 3.5% if your campaign succeeds in 30 or 60 days. All campaigns must raise a minimum of $500 to be funded. Pubslush has a list of vetted editors, designers and marketing professionals for their authors to use out of their Pubslush funding. They are also the publisher of your book. Without an account with them, I was unable to find out what the royalties are with Pubslush.

CHAPTER 5

Building an Author Platform

Pre-existing Business Platform

One of the most common questions I get from business owners who are expanding into becoming published authors is whether they should use their existing company website as their platform or start a new one. In my opinion, start a new platform as an author.

An author platform is used to create visibility and authority to reach to a target audience. All of the aspects of an author platform should direct your audience back to your branded website. A platform can include social media, email newsletter, a body of published work, speaking engagements, YouTube or podcasts, a tribe, membership in organizations, awards, recurring media appearances or interviews and a branded website.

Keep two things in mind. First, your readers might not be fans of your current business or interested in weeding through your current site to find what they are interested in. Second, there is always a possibility that you might sell your current business. Even if that idea is the furthest thing from your mind at the time, you should plan for the possibility.

I had a huge following on Facebook, Twitter and my company blog, but because I didn't plan in advance, I lost those connections when I sold my company. Had I been blogging on my popular blog about my new blog, tweeting about my author Twitter handle and inviting people to "Like" my new Facebook page, I would not have needed to start from scratch in my new venture. I'm not complaining, I'm just advising you to learn from my experience.

Author Websites

You should have an author website and social media presence before you publish your book. Building a platform should be happening simultaneously with your book writing. Launching a website and joining the social media world just in time to launch is like showing up two days after a potluck to an empty banquet room with your food in hand. You might have the best potluck dish in the history of potluck dinners, but no one is around to enjoy it.

If you don't have an author website and social media presence, you limit your ability to sell your book. You will resort to hoping folks will stumble upon you and buy your book. It is like having a store on Main Street with no signage and a locked door.

Blogging 101

You might be sitting in front of your computer with a document open wondering what to do now that you're officially a blogger. I remember when I first started blogging in 2007. What stands out is how LONG it took me to produce each blog post. It was a slow and drawn out process because I was unfamiliar with it. Now I can have a blog up in a matter of minutes or at least less than an hour depending on the topic. It is overwhelming at first but it gets super easy.

Most of your social media branding should be designed to lead directly to your website. You are going to need to keep your website fresh by maintaining your blog with new content appearing on a regular basis. Your blog should have the consumer one click away from being on Amazon using your affiliate link to buy your book.

If Facebook, Twitter, Google+ and the other social media tools go down in a blaze of fire, you will have your blog to fall back on. Imagine if you were counting on MySpace several years ago as your main connection with your consumers and then suddenly it turned into a ghost town as people abandoned their profiles for greener pastures.

Your blog and newsletter are the goal posts you are trying to bring everyone through when on Twitter or Facebook.

The best place to get started is to look at really successful bloggers and see what they are doing. I have provided a list of helpful blog sites in the back of the book to get you started.

Never Apologize—I told you to create a schedule and stick to it However, I know that things will happen in life. There will be weeks that you miss, maybe even months, if something major occurs in your life. When you get back to writing your blog, don't apologize for being absent. Just pick up and start blogging. It is okay if your comeback story is about what happened over the period of time that you were missing, but don't apologize. Some people will find your blog randomly and start reading it in the middle of your blogging career so don't annoy those people by making the first blog post they find your apology letter.

Define your Niche—What makes you special? What are you passionate about and what will help convince readers that you are an expert in your field? Think about those things when you define your niche. Your niche shouldn't be so narrow that only a tiny portion of the population can relate or find your information useful. Think about the topic of the current book you are writing and the next 10 books you have planned. For instance, I post food recipes on my blog because in my next 10 books I have at least one cookbook planned.

Be Useful—Provide content that will be helpful to your readers. You may have to play around with it for a bit until you find your strength. I used to write a motivational blog and newsletter that hit mailboxes every Thursday morning. I wasn't sure if they were working until letters from readers started trickling in telling me how much they counted on their Thursday morning newsletter with a cup of coffee in hand. As time progressed, I got some of the most amazing, heartfelt and personal emails from my readers. Make your posts entertaining, educational, informative and/or inspiring.

Keep it Short—As often as you can, keep your blog posts short. I always start generously cutting when the rough draft of my blog jumps over the 500 word mark. Sometimes it is hard to keep a topic that short, so consider whether the blog could be broken up into a series of two or three blogs. If the length is necessary, you can make a long post seem shorter. You can break up the bulky appearance by using bullets, subtitles, and short sentences inside short paragraphs of 4 to 5 sentences.

Use Catchy Titles—The title of your blog is what is going to inspire people to click over to your website from the comfort of their social media living room. Your title needs to engage them and make them want to make the leap. Keep the titles SEO (Search Engine Optimization) friendly by making each title 64 characters or less. This length makes your title fit inside the clickable phrase in search results.

SEO Friendly—After you write your rough draft, use Google AdWords Keyword Tool to find what key words or phrases in your blog post have the highest Global Monthly Search Volume. If you need to change a word to a similar word that is more search friendly, by all means do it. Use those keywords as your tags on your blog as well.

Use Tags—Tags are used by search engines to index content on websites. Originally websites used mostly hidden keywords to get the highest ranking from search engines, but that no longer works. Search engines have improved their algorithms to ignore these hidden keywords. Tags are currently (but remember everything changes fast) a great method for Search Engine Optimization. Tags are keywords for each blog post you create. They should be short two or three word phrases. Using tags is the best way to bring total strangers to your blog. Tags are easy to add to blogs. Look for the "tags" box and put single words or phrases separated by a comma inside the "add" box.

Use a SEO Plug-in—An example is All in One SEO Pack, which is available on WordPress and is programmed to optimize your blog.

Make Sharing Easy—Every blogging platform has a whole host of widgets you can use to make sharing easy. You want it to be easy for the reader to share your content. It is smart to have sharing buttons at the top of your blog post and again at the bottom of your post. Some people will automatically hit "Like" within the first few lines of your post and others will wait until they have read the entire post before deciding to share. Your goal should be to make it easy to share for both types of readers!

Be Transparent—Just keep it real. Don't go out into the blogosphere attempting to look super human with no flaws. Some of my most popular blog posts are the vulnerable ones that showed my failures, flaws and faults and a valuable life lesson. "Fake it till you make it" is not the motto of blogging. Being transparent allows people to know you for who you really are with all of your strengths and weaknesses showing.

Don't Over Analyze—Have fun blogging and don't over think every post to the point of being sick with worry. If you feel a bit uneasy about something you have written for your blog, sleep on it. In the morning, if you still want to post it, ask a trusted friend or adviser to read it and see if you are being snarky, sarcastic or rude. Sometimes when something isn't sitting right with you it is for a good reason, but don't paralyze yourself over it.

Appearance Counts—Use a photograph in every blog post. It breaks up the content and makes the page look good. You can get free pictures and use free photo editing sites. I take the most random photographs now, with the thought that someday I might need a photograph of a STOP sign that is weathered. I have a huge library of random photographs to use and sometimes I just take a quick one on my iPhone to fit an article I am working on. When you can't make something work, head to the free photo websites and find one that does. My virtual assistant, Jennifer Smith, set me up with a plug-in on WordPress called PhotoDropper that is my new favorite source.

Have a Search Window—I love search windows on blogs. Never have a blog or website without one. A reader might be visiting your blog because they followed a link to a recipe. If they are impressed with your recipe, they may want to search your site for other recipes. Even if you have a category called recipes, they will most likely use the search box to go directly to what they are looking for.

Link to Your Books—Provide a static column on your blog that consistently has images of your books with a link to them on Amazon using your Amazon Associate code. Make it easy for your blog visitor to buy your book when they decide that they like you. Any time you talk about your book in a blog post, you should link to your book on Amazon.

Links Open on a Separate Page—One of my biggest pet peeves is clicking on a link in a blog post, and having it replace what I was reading. It is better to have it open in a separate window, so the reader can leave it open and go back to the original content. Once I finish reading a blog post, I like to jump around and read what links the author recommended. Having links open in separate windows makes returning to your blog an easy experience for your readers.

Be a Good Neighbor in the Blogosphere—If you want people to come read your blog and leave comments, the best habit to get into is going to other people's blogs and leaving comments.

Have a Comment Policy—There are truly some mean people out there in the world who don't have anything better to do than to surf the Internet looking for people to tear down. Don't let them get you down. Set a policy for what you will tolerate in your blog comments, because your blog is your house. Hold to the policy and delete comments that are rude, abusive or vulgar. All blog platforms have an option to moderate comments before they post.

Subscribers—Make it easy for people to subscribe to your blog. When they subscribe to your blog, they receive a notification in their inboxes each time you post a blog.

Don't Invite Readers to an Empty Blog—Either spend a month practicing blogging before you make your grand entrance, or backdate 4 to 10 blogs as you build your blog. This way people have something to look at while they are on your site for the first time. You can promote all those backdated posts in between your fresh content on social media.

Ask Questions—Ask your reader questions in your blog post to encourage interaction.

Email Newsletters

Email newsletters are a key marketing tool because they allow you to have a little black book of past, present and potential clients. Getting an email address from a customer is huge because they have invited you into their lives via their most precious inbox.

A newsletter should be sent on a regular schedule. When you are starting out, 1 to 2 times per month is plenty. You don't want to be cluttering up their inboxes with daily or weekly newsletters until you have something to offer them every week. You can use pictures, linked to the blog posts you wrote since the last newsletter, and share your progress on your newest project. You can create, send and track email newsletters using MailChimp, Constant Contact, Emma, iContact, AWeber, or other newsletter platforms.

Main Street America

The social media frontier is the single most cost-effective means of increasing sales that is available in the market today. If you don't have a blog, newsletter, YouTube channel, Twitter account, or Facebook page you are losing thousands of contacts per day. Consumers are living their lives out on the Internet. They make purchasing decisions, form loyal relationships and spread incredible word-of-mouth advertising on the Internet.

There is a conversation happening online. Word-of-mouth advertising and many other opportunities abound in the virtual marketplace of social media. More than any other marketing method in the course of history, the arena of social networking gives author-preneurs the upper hand over having a PR firm or publicist run social media campaigns for well-known authors. Social media is about person to person contact that is sincere, personal and transparent. The intimate atmosphere that naturally occurs in social networking creates abundant opportunities to influence untapped readers.

An important step in setting up your social media empire is to add your picture and bio during the set up phase. Too many people postpone this step and lose potential followers because of it. The Twitter egg profile picture and the Facebook silhouette make it look like no one is home and tells consumers that you must not care about your brand.

Social Media Stats as of March 2015

- Facebook—Over 1.44 billion active users and 1.25 billion mobile active users.
- Twitter—More than 302 million active users and over 500 million Tweets sent per day.
- LinkedIn—364 million total users.
- Pinterest—47 million users.
- Google Plus—2.2 billion profiles but only 9% actively post public content. There were Internet rumors of the demise of Google Plus in March 2015. Bradley Horowitz said, "No,

Google Plus is not dead. In fact, it's got more signs of life than it's had in sometime."

- Goodreads—30 million users.
- Instagram—300 million active users and 75 million daily users.

All of this information will be outdated in a minute, because all the social media sites are constantly growing. Social media is moving that fast, and you simply have to be part of it to keep up with it.

Small businesses are no longer slaves of the once most important factor in business, "location, location, location." Authors are no longer forced to use brick-and-mortar stores to sell their books. Whether your business is on Main Street America, in your home or on Corporate Lane USA, the new mantra is "Google, Yahoo or Bing search-ability."

In a room full of small businesses, authors and multi-million dollar corporations, the most common excuse I have heard is, "We don't have time for social networking." With the culture of consumers changing every single day to the online community at an alarming rate, every company must make the time to follow their customers to the Internet.

The excuse that comes in at a close second is, "We don't know how to use social networking." There are tutorials and blogs all over Internet that will teach any company the basics of joining the online conversation. Another method is to spend a few days on the sidelines watching some active user's methods.

The fact is that if you haven't joined the online conversation, then you cannot direct the conversation toward your books. The Internet is today's Main Street America. An author that does not have a blog, newsletter, Facebook page, or Twitter account is literally doing business without a storefront in today's society. Consumers are readily available for direct one-on-one contact with authors. Join the conversation and direct the conversation toward your website.

Think ahead as you build your platform. Keep in mind the book you are working on now as well as the additional books you may write in the future.

Promoting Your Book using Social Media

Promotion of your book should start long before you finish it. Talk about your project, research, writers block, breakthroughs, defeats and triumphs as you work on your book. Engage people on your blog and social media campaigns in the process of writing your book. Track and share your word count progress. Being transparent in your writing process will not only generate interest in your book, but it will also make others feel personally invested in your book because they have been "with you" every step of the way.

Some authors have successfully created buzz about their book launch by getting all of their fans and supporters to buy their book on the same day so that it shoots up the ratings rank immediately. Being ranked highly increases the chances of strangers learning about your book. In 2008, Alex and Brett Harris successfully pulled off what they called a Book Bomb. On the first day of publication their book, *Do Hard Things,* hit the Top 5 on the Amazon.com Bestseller List. It stunned the publishing world that a non-fiction hardcover book for teens could sell, at all, let alone reach the Top 5 list. Their book calls for teens to rebel against low expectations.

Their campaign was so successful that they did it again in 2010. They provided web banners, widgets, sample email blasts and blog posts free to anyone who wanted to help them spread their message. It was a brilliant grassroots campaign that all authors can learn from. I've provided their web address in the back of the book so you can follow these dynamic brothers.

Domain Registrar

Your first step to creating your platform is to do a search on one of many domain registrar websites like GoDaddy, Domain.com, NameCheap or Name to see if your name is available to use as a domain name for your author website. For the most part, you are going to want to use your own name or pen name for your platform. My domain name is KaylaFioravanti.com. I hemmed and hawed about whether to come up with a cute domain name that was easier to spell than Fioravanti, but the reality is that if someone is looking for me as an author they are going to be looking for my name.

There are exceptions to using your name as the domain. For instance, I recently purchased GogoNaughtyPaws.com for a series of children's books I am writing with my daughters about our very naughty cat named Gogo. My regular readers and subscribers would not enjoy me posting, blogging and talking non-stop about my cat. But cat lovers and Gogo fans would love to hear about him on a regular basis. For that reason, I created a separate platform for that series of books. I still talk about my cat, but he isn't the sole focus of what I talk about.

Simply plug your name into a domain registrar and see if it is available. If it isn't, you might have to get creative. You can also see who owns your name, and find out whether it is being used and if they will sell it to you. Some people are totally fair and will sell you the domain for a tiny profit, and some people are crazy and will ask for thousands of dollars. There is a domain name out there that I want and the owners aren't responding. I have simply set an alarm in my calendar to remind me to watch it when their purchase expires. It is best to know up front if you need to use your middle initial or come up with a name that will encompass your brand.

It is worthwhile to buy up domain names that you think you might use in the future. It isn't very expensive to buy a domain name for two years and let it lapse if you choose not to use it.

If purchasing your domain is financially out of the question, you do have the option of using a custom domain (i.e. Yourname.com) or hosting on your blog platform like BlogSpot, Typepad or WordPress (i.e.Yourname.wordpress.com) which will save you the cost of purchasing your domain. I do recommend making purchase of your domain a high priority so that you own it, just in case you become a household name as an author.

Hosting

After you buy your domain, you will need to choose a web host to make your website accessible on the Internet. I use Eco-Office Gals because I like supporting small business owners and they were highly recommended. There are a variety of small web hosting companies available or you can pick one of the big companies including Ipage, JustHost, Web.com, GoDaddy, Host Gator, Hub, InMotion, GreenGeeks or many others. To choose the right web host for you consider disk space and bandwidth needs based on graphics, pages and traffic; pricing; 24-hour 7-day a week customer support; in-house security department; standard cPanel hosting; website speed; WordPress knowledge; and the ability to install and support scripts.

Website Fundamentals

WordPress is the perfect platform for your author website. You can use WordPress for all of your needs as a static website and/or blog. It is simple and easy to use. I don't enjoy learning how to use the newest widgets the computer world has to offer. If I could, I would probably just use the computer as a glorified typewriter and skip all the fancy bells and whistles that technology adds on.

When we owned our last company, we had a tech expert who could do everything and anything related to technology. I learned as little as possible to get by. But reality hit when we sold our company, and I was faced with running my own little business without tech support. A teardrop fell here and there as I faced each new challenge. Several times I whined, "I miss Alex" in front of my computer. But I survived and so can you.

I partly survived by turning over all the things that hurt my head to think about to my virtual assistant. I normally take a swing at figuring it out on my own first then I send out a cry for help. There are things that simply drain the creativity out of me and aren't worth trying to do myself. Most of my emails or instant messages to my virtual assistant, Jennifer go like this, "Ugh, I tried to ______ but _____! I need your help!" She quotes me a price and by that point it is worth every penny.

I started out as a blogger using Typepad. Everyt' the advice I got from others was that I needed to use ᵥ. my new website. Thankfully, when I arrived at the backend o. new WordPress blog I found it was beyond easy to navigate. It is possible to follow the steps given in WordPress to set up your own site. But keep in mind that this is going to be where people get their first impression of you.

My gifting is not in web design, so I always hire the setting up portion of my website to someone else. Those emails to Jennifer go like this, "I have this idea. I want to ______. Can you do it?" To which she responds by saying yes, giving me a price and some ideas of her own that fill in the technology side of my website.

If hiring someone to set up your website is out of the question financially, I recommend that you set up an account with WordPress, Typepad (not a free platform) or Blogger. Spend some time going through the information they offer once you have signed in. Shop around for the one that looks doable to you by checking out their templates, videos and information. Keep in mind that your average teenager can be hired to do your web design. I think their brains came equipped with an extra plug-in at birth that wires them to naturally understand technology beyond our wildest dreams.

Facebook Fundamentals

Most people already have a Facebook profile. If you don't, then signing up for a Facebook account is step number one for you. Your Facebook profile is not going to be your business page. There are several reasons why you need to have a separate Facebook page to use for your business. A Facebook profile only allows you to have 5000 friends which may seem like a lot now, but down the road, it will limit you.

Benefits of a Business Facebook Page

- Number of "Likes" is limitless.

- Run ads.
- Promote updates.
- Track traffic including organic, paid and viral reach.
- Track trends including "Likes," people talking about and weekly total reach.
- Helps you make business decisions based on traffic.
- Easier for others to share your updates from mobile devices.
- Available author app.
- Legitimizes author when link goes to a business page instead of a personal page from website.
- Build audience via traditional email, private messages, ads and sharing pages.
- Easily managed from your computer and/or "pages" app on smart phones.
- Use a Facebook widget on your website.
- Vanity Facebook URLs are available.

Setting up Your Facebook Business Page

Facebook changes and updates how it works all the time. I'm going to give you a general roadmap that should get you to the right section.

- Look for either "pages" or "create a page" and click on it. If you clicked on "pages," you should see "create a page" and should click on that.
- Several categories will come up. You want to choose "artist, band or public figure" or whatever category they have at the moment that fits an author.
- Next click on category and author should show up and click on it.
- Put in your name and agree to Facebook Page Terms.
- Upload your profile picture.
- Add your bio in the about and your website.
- Once redirected to your new page hit "Like" to like your own page.

- You should add a cover photo.
- After this, you are prepared to start adding content, building an audience, creating ads.
- Good first steps include adding events and milestones, and putting up photo albums from the status update box.
- Create a vanity URL for your Facebook Page. Go to http://www.Facebook.com/username. Pick the username that Facebook suggests or create your own. Select Check availability to see if the username you want is available. If it is, click Confirm to confirm your choice.
- Select your preferred method and frequency of notifications by going to Account Settings and then clicking on Notifications. Open up each device method and make your selections.

Facebook Ads

I know you hear people complaining about seeing ads on Facebook, but they must not mind all that much because Facebook ads work. Whenever I run a month long $50 ad for one of my books on Facebook I see the sales for that book double for the month. That more than pays for itself, gives me exposure and more potential for word-of-mouth advertising.

Ads are easy to create once you have your author page set up. Simply go to "create an ad" and get started. You can choose your target market specifically, to age group, location, gender, precise interests, broad categories, connections, language, workplace, relationship status and education level. You can set your campaign budget with either a per-day cap or a lifetime budget. Facebook will suggest a bid to pay per CPM (which stands for Costs per Mile but really just means clicks), but I always bid lower. I never put in a campaign budget higher than $50 because I want to see if it works and tweak it based on what I learn.

Promote Updates

You can promote your updates for a nominal charge. I have tried it out a few times with $1 and $5 bids to promote an update. It is worth it if your update either increases your traffic on your blog or helps you sell more books. Once you have enough "Likes" on your page, Facebook will start offering you the ability to promote an update. Currently the magic number for Facebook to offer the "promote this post" option is 100 "Likes."

Tracking Trends and Traffic

Facebook makes it easy to track trends. From your personal page you can see how many people "Liked" or commented on your update, but that doesn't really tell you how many people you reached. Lots of people are Facebook lurkers. They just watch what happens on Facebook, but never hit "Like" or leave a comment. I often meet people who tell me that they love my updates about my pets, but I thought that they weren't even hanging out on Facebook since I never saw them update, comment or "Like." Lurkers are good, but on a personal page hard to track.

On your business page, you can see how many people saw your update including how many were organic, viral or paid. An organic view of your Facebook posts tells you how many people who "Like" your page saw your update. Viral views of your Facebook posts are viewers who do not "Like" your page but saw your post because someone they know shared, "Liked" or commented on your update. Paid views lets you know how many views you received from promoting your update. I have found this tool to be immensely helpful.

I work from home so I often put up pictures of my pets since they are my only company while I work. My cat Gogo always receives a lot of attention and "Likes." I had several suggestions to write a book about him and get him his own Facebook page. I decided to get him his own page and see what the interest might be for a book. What I learned was fascinating. Cats sell, cats go viral and my cat has better potential on Facebook than I do.

Stats don't Lie

- Gogo Naughty Paws page has 5x less "Likes" than mine
- Gogo Naughty Paws gets 2-4x more organic views than mine
- Gogo Naughty Paws has 4-6x more viral views than my page

I'm so fascinated by the potential of the cat market that I've even become a professional member of the Cat Writers Association.

Twitter Fundamentals

Twitter can be like trying to drink water out of a fire hose. It is fast paced microblogging. Twitter has changed over the years from when they first started to make some things easier and other things harder. When I first joined twitter as @EssentialU, it was very easy to quickly get over 10,000 followers. Gaining followers is one of the things Twitter has made harder. When I sold my company, the @EssentialU Twitter handle went with it and I started building @KaylaFioravanti following from scratch.

You could build a following by following a ton of people. They would follow you back and you could quickly build a following. But now Twitter requires that your following to follower ratio not go above a certain threshold. I am constantly seeing people ask, "Why can't I follow more than 2000 people?" The answer is that you can't go over 2000 until the ratio of who is following you back, is smaller. This leaves you forced to unfollow people who don't follow you back, which isn't the easiest task on earth because from your computer you have to click through to each person you follow to see if they are following you back. That is slow and time consuming.

Proper Twitter etiquette is to follow back everyone and anyone who follows you. If you don't follow back, you will eventually lose that follower when they get annoyed that your relationship is only one sided or they hit the follower/following ratio window. Social media is a relationship based building block for your business. If you don't have the time or inclination to follow people back, then you are simply using it as a "me, me, me" tool to promote you and only you.

When someone addresses you on Twitter, always be sure to send a reply. You can see who is talking to or about you on Twitter by clicking on the @Connect button. Direct messaging has become cluttered with automated messages saying things like, "Thanks for following me, click here to __" It all reads like impersonal spam and most people on Twitter don't even check their Direct Messages anymore.

If you want to start a conversation with someone use their Twitter handle when you compose a Tweet. For instance, you could Tweet me by saying, "@KaylaFioravanti I just read your new book *How to Self-Publish, A Guide for Author-preneurs* and loved it! #howto #author" I promise I will not only reply, but will also retweet it.

What is retweet? Retweeting is another easy way to win friends on Twitter. When you read content that you like simply hit the Retweet button that will appear when you hover the mouse just anywhere on a specific Tweet.

How to build your Following

- Use Twitter Advertising for Promoted Tweets and Promoted Accounts
- Run contests from your blog for Twitter followers
- Add yourself to directories like Twiends, WeFollow and Twellow
- Add a Twitter Widget to your website
- Retweet and interact with the people you follow
- Use #Hashtags
- Follow people in your field

What to Tweet

Now that you are on Twitter, you will master the art of speaking in 140 characters or less. To successfully use Twitter, you need to learn how to keep it short. Tweet about your day, what you just read, tweet quotes and pictures, retweet other people and, above all, use hashtags. Unlike Facebook, you can be repetitive on Twitter because the content is constantly moving every minute. To promote my website, I will often schedule a tweet that has a link to a specific blog post up to four times in a week or month.

Hashtags

The use of hashtags is one of the changes on Twitter that makes it easier. The symbol # followed immediately by a word or group of words is a hashtag, for example #foodie or #whatwasithinking. The trends of hashtags are constantly changing. One day the biggest hashtag might be #presidentialdebates2013 and the next day it might be #justinbieberisalegend. These hashtags are used to categorize tweets and follow tweeters that you are interested in.

Hashtags are used to engage in Twitter conversations, find relevant people to follow and gain valuable social media insight and engage in Trending Topics. You can look up current hashtags, find hashtags to follow and even define a hashtag by going to Hashtags.org or Twubs.com.

Hashtags can be used in the middle of a tweet or at the end of a tweet or both. Using one to two hashtags per tweet is plenty. You can test out other hashtags by tweeting your message again later with new ones.

You can empower your tribe to promote your content by creating a brand-able media-rich landing page when you register your own hashtag using Twubs.com. Use a combination of your customized and trending hashtags to get the widest audience.

Examples of Tweets

Written from "compose a tweet"

This is a great #recipe for chicken chili http://kaylafioravanti.com/mean-chicken-chili-recipe/#foodie

Or I shorten the URL in the tweet by using TinyURL.com (or bitly.com)
This is a great #recipe for chicken chili http://tinyurl.com/bzrwbv5 #foodie

Or directly from the blog post and add the hashtags at the end
Mean Chicken Chili Recipe: http://kaylafioravanti.com/mean-chicken-chili-recipe/ #recipe #foodie

Scheduling Tweets

You can use third-party platforms to schedule and manage your tweets. I like to use Twuffer to schedule tweets of quotes and blogs I've written in the past. You can also use Hootsuite, FutureTweets, Tweetdeck, 14blocks, Dynamictweets, Autotweeter, LaterBro, Tweetsqueue or many other apps you will find if you enter the search words "how to schedule a tweet" into your search engine.

Using third-party platforms for Twitter won't reduce your visibility at this point in history, but on Facebook it could. Facebook is constantly changing what information you see from your friends and companies that you have "Like." I suggest always using Facebook from Facebook.

Some of these third-party tools only do future tweets and some can manage your Twitter or social media empire. Spend some time looking around and find a tool that works best for you. Just be sure that you don't rely so heavily on the tool that you forget to follow people back.

LinkedIn Fundamentals

LinkedIn is the business development meeting place. It is all about making business connections, finding jobs, employees, special interest groups and recommendations. LinkedIn is a great place to find resources and references to people who can help you as you build your brand. You can also use it to promote your books and expertise. By using the Groups, Jobs and Companies drop down menus, you will quickly be on your way to connecting with businesses and individuals.

Google+ Fundamentals

Lately I've seen more and more Facebook updates that go something like this, "I don't like the new update on Facebook. I'm thinking of moving over to Google+." That alone is a good reason to be active on Google+ because as people get annoyed with Facebook's many changes, and they look for what is new, hot and easy to use. Google+ has it all.

From Google+ you can write long updates, embed video, share photographs, create a hangout, follow trends, join communities, find people, play games and share events. The ability to write long updates has inspired some people to use Google+ as their blog platform. The ability to navigate easily to Google for searches, maps, images, your calendar, your Gmail, YouTube and more make Google+ a very attractive addition or alternative to Facebook.

Goodreads Fundamentals

Goodreads is a community of readers. You first sign yourself up as a user and then you can set yourself up as an author in their community. It is a great place to interact with and be found by readers. Once your book is available for sale, you can look for it on Goodreads. If it doesn't show up, request to be a librarian and add it yourself.

As you set up your author page, you will have the option of having your Blog feed directly into Goodreads. Whenever I see this option, I jump at it. It becomes another platform in which new readers can find you.

You can run ads for your books in this community, but make sure your genre is one that has a large following in Goodreads. I learned this one the hard way by creating an ad for my book, *How to Make Melt & Pour Soap Base from Scratch* in Goodreads. The ads are pre-paid and as you get clicks on your ad, it subtracts money from your pre-paid account. That ad might be running in Goodreads for the next 10 years because there are not a large number of soap makers in the community of Goodreads.

The best opportunity on Goodreads is to run a book giveaway when your book is released. You have one free opportunity within one year of the release of your book. You can set how long the giveaway runs and the number of copies you will give away. This is a great way to increase interest and to get people connected to your book; I ran a one month giveaway promotion and gave away 10 books. Next time, I will give away more books because Goodread readers are pretty faithful about giving reviews on Goodreads and Amazon. You risk getting a bad review because there are no guarantees, but the low cost PR is well worth it.

On Goodreads you technically can respond to bad reviews, but I don't suggest it. No matter how good your book is there will be people out there who can and will find fault in it. Don't take it personally and don't go around trying to defend your book to bad reviews. The best response to a bad review is a good review from someone else. Ask for reviews. I will talk more about that later in this book.

Note: Amazon announced the purchase of Goodreads on March 28, 2013.

Pinterest Fundamentals

I let out a big sigh when I started getting invites to join Pinterest. I thought, "Oh please not another social media site to manage!" But I learned long ago that you should always reserve your name on any new-fangled social media site that shows up. Better that you own it, put up a bio and pictures and then park on it then have someone else using it for something totally unrelated to what you do.

Pinterest is used to share photographs, ideas, craft projects, recipes and so forth. When you set up your account, you create boards that are interesting to you and are part of your branding. Pinterest will grab the photograph used in your blog posts and stay linked so if someone is really interested in the recipe you just blogged, they can click through to your website. The point of Pinterest is to pin, repin, follow and share.

Author Central on Amazon

Author Central puts your social media efforts right into the shopping mammoth that is Amazon. Author Central puts an author profile on Amazon that you can use to reach more readers, share about yourself, track sales and include your bio, photographs, videos and Twitter feed. You can even connect readers to your author blog.

Other Social Media

Tumblr, MySpace, Instagram, Ning, Pheed and the list is constantly expanding and contracting. Are you wondering why I included MySpace? The old is new again with a facelift for MySpace. Don't feel like you have to be the master of all social media sites, but reserve your name in all of them in case it becomes hot, and to keep others unrelated to you, from using it.

Linking Updates between Social Media Platforms

I just listed a ton of social media sites for you to set yourself up on. You might be feeling really overwhelmed and thinking of linking the same updates on all of the sites. This is doable in the setup of your account or through third party hosts. Just make sure that you are speaking the right language for the connected sites. My pet peeve is seeing someone only talk in Twitter language with hashtags throughout their update on Facebook. It screams, "I don't spend time here!" Just be thoughtful as you make your updating link decisions.

Note: At the end of March 2013 news reports started surfacing that Facebook is considering incorporating hashtags to improve how business owners and entrepreneurs network. As of July 2015, this Facebook feature has been introduced on Facebook, but can only show you a post shared with you and is not available to everyone.

Teenagers and Google

If you get lost, overwhelmed or stuck, the two best free resources you can tap into are Google and a teenager. If you don't know how to do something, just Google it! Simply go to Google.com and input your question into the search box. You will find videos, experts and how-to instructions on just about any topic you may have. I use Google for everything. From technical things, such as adding a copyright symbol in Word, to fire alarms going off in my house for no reason, to how to unlock a locked bathroom door with a specific kind of handle. I did all those searches recently and found the answer.

If the answer you find on Google makes your head hurt, the next best step is to ask a teenager. They might roll their eyes or snicker at you for not knowing how to do something that to them is basic and simple, but they will either know how to do it or will be able to figure it out quickly.

CHAPTER 6

Budgeting Time

Are you wondering how much time it will take to write your book? The answer really depends on how fast you write and how focused you can be.

As I mentioned previously things didn't go as planned when I wrote *How to Make Melt & Pour Soap Base from Scratch*. My plan to take five months turned into a six week race to the finish line.

The Art, Science and Business of Aromatherapy took me just over a month to write, edit, re-edit, and fix with the help of expert criticism. It was a monster of a technical book and the hardest one I have written. Writing it was more than a full time job. I worked day and night on it.

I wrote *DIY Kitchen Chemistry* in just one week. This book was fast because it was only a matter of organizing information and recipes that I had previously provided on YouTube and my blog. Editing and layout took another week. By the time I got through this third book, I was a pro! I even came in ahead of my scheduled December 31st 'drop dead' deadline.

I got the idea to write the book you are reading in February 2013 on an Indie Mastermind Cruise. I sat down to start writing it from scratch on March 7, 2013. In between traveling and a super busy month with my kids, I managed to send it out for editing by March 18. I went through two rounds of editing until April 12. I submitted the book to CreateSpace on April 17, received my proof April 19 and made edits the same day. The book was online on April 22.

A short time frame takes dedication and focus. There can be a personal price to pay as well. When I am in that zone, my family eats a lot of pizza and the house is a bit neglected. In the end, though, the books get finished faster.

Gleaning from Your Expertise

In reality, it took me years in the cosmetic industry to gain the expertise to formulate the long held industry secret recipes I shared in my first three books. My poetry book, *When I was Young I Flew the Sun Like a Kite* took a few weeks to organize and publish, but the poems included in the book were written over a twenty-five year span. This book is the product of publishing eight books in four years.

The time it took to write, edit and publish my books may have been short, but the time it took to learn the lessons and gain the necessary expertise can be counted in years.

NaNoWriMo

National Novel Writing Month (NaNoWriMo) is a very motivating opportunity for writers. I highly suggest joining the November session, or the April and July sessions of Camp NaNoWriMo to kick start your writing. During NaNoWriMo, you commit to writing 50,000 words in one month in your book. It does not matter what kind of book you are writing.

I wrote the first draft of my book *Puffy & Blue* during the November 2012 NaNoWriMo session. Committing to something publicly is a huge motivator for most people. I wrote 51,660 words in my first NaNoWriMo and I plan on participating in future events. When you join, be sure to look for me so we can be writing buddies for NaNoWriMo or cabin mates at Camp NaNoWriMo.

NaNoWriMo is a great motivator, but please don't wait to get started until November, April or July. If the timing is right, you should do it, but if you are reading this book and would have to wait to jump on the NaNoWriMo bandwagon then by all means don't wait! Really, just get started now! If now is when you are investigating writing a book, then now is the right time to get started.

The End is Quick

Once your book is written, edited and the layout and cover design are finalized, the wait is nearly over. CreateSpace works amazingly fast. After you submit your files, you simply need to wait for approval, order a proof, review your proof, fix any last minute errors and resubmit your files. I have never made any major changes that caused me to order a second proof however, if there were big changes in the book or on the cover I would. Once you approve your proof, it normally takes 24 to 48 hours for your book to become available online at Amazon.

While you are waiting for your book to show up on Amazon, you can take your finished work directly over from CreateSpace to Kindle Direct Publishing and start the process over there.

The Long and Short of It

On the long side of budgeting time, give yourself a year and on the short side of budgeting time, give yourself at least three months. If writing your book will take more than one year then you simply must set goals to reach each month. If your deadline is too far away you will struggle to ever reach it.

CHAPTER 7

The Importance of Editing

> "It is perfectly okay to write garbage—as long as you edit brilliantly."
> C. J. Cherryh

Every author needs an editor or two. Even if you are the King or Queen of grammar, you still need an editor. As the writer, you are too close to your work to see the errors that will jump right out to your editing team; or worse—your readers!

Crowdsource

Whatever you do, make sure your book goes through more than two sets of eyes (yours and your editor's) because you both become too familiar with your words to catch simple mistakes. The best case scenario is to have a copy editor and a content editor. I like to have my work go to the content editor first to move things around, change the flow, catch flaws in my logic and then go to a copy editor to fix the grammar.

Sources for free or low cost editing include: crowdsourcing on your social media platforms, English teachers, other authors, professional editors moonlighting in their off hours, CreateSpace editors and/or family, friends and amateur editors.

For this book, I tested out crowdsourcing editing. To find volunteer editors I wrote this Facebook post:

> Anyone interested in being a beta-tester on my book *How to Self-Publish*? I am looking to crowdsource the first draft in order to get fresh eyes that catch what I missed, constructive criticism and editing, and feedback on how I can improve the information and so forth.

I got 32 offers, 32 people agreed to my contract and 27 people delivered edited copies of my book on time. Of those I got countless ideas, insightful questions and 2,821 corrections. Crowdsource editing was more time consuming for me during the editing process than hiring an editor, but the insight and perspective of 27 different people with various degrees of experience using social media, blogging, formatting in Word and other areas I covered in this book was priceless. My second round of editing was done by 10 people who stuck with me to the end.

I sent all of my crowdsourced editors the following private Facebook message:

> Dear____,
> I am really excited about the group of crowdsourced editors that volunteered to work on this project with me. I expect to be ready to send it on either Sunday or Monday and will be asking for a 7–10 day turn-around time.
>
> I just have a few housekeeping duties to handle first.
>
> 1. Please respond back with your regular email address.
> 2. Please reply back to me in the affirmative that you agree to the following: I will not share Kayla's manuscript with anyone else during or after the editing process in any form. I understand that there are no fees being paid to

> crowdsourced editors. My payment will be a social media thank you, mention in the book as one of my crowdsourced editor, early insider information, a signed copy of the finished book and Kayla's undying gratitude.

The manuscript will be emailed to you in Word with "track changes" turned on. You can edit for grammar, content, make changes and give any suggestions that you have. I am not married to the title of the book, chapter headings or the flow of the book.

I am asking for a 7–10 day turn-around time for two reasons. First, I am on a tight deadline to finish the book in time for a speaking engagement in early May. Second, it is human nature is to put everything off to the last moment. If someone gave me a month for a deadline I would put it off to the last days anyway. Anything earlier than 7 days would be thrilling for me.

Thank you so much,

Kayla

Editing using Word and Google Documents

After I emailed out 32 copies of my manuscript for editing, I wondered how in the world I was going organize all the input so that I could review and absorb all the input. Thankfully, Word made it amazingly simple.

Once all of your edited copies have been returned to you, save each by clicking "save as" into a special folder with each editor's name saved into the document title. Go to "review" and click on "compare" and choose "combine" in the drop down menu. In the "original document" box put in your copy of the manuscript and in the "revise document" box put in the first edited copy of your book. Below the "revise document" box you will see "label changes with" Put the name of the editor in the version you are merging in. Below you will see boxes to use to decide what changes you want shown and click on the appropriate boxes. Pick show changes at "Word level" and show changes in "original document."

Google offers a simple method for editing as well. You can use Google Documents to create a single document that you share with a group of editors. If you use Gmail already or any Google product simply sign in and go to "drive" along the top menu, click on "create" and using the drop down menu, click on "document." Once a document appears, you can copy and paste your book into the new Google Document. Click on "share" and Google will automatically pop up a window to name and save the document. The next window will allow you to put in the email addresses of your editors under "add people." Leave yourself as the owner and be sure that you are set on "private" access so that only the people you list can get into the document.

The nice thing about using a Google Document is that you won't have to merge the comments. All comments, corrections and efforts will be visible to everyone in the group. The negative side is that all the other comments might distract from or discourage aggressive editing.

Printed Version

You can do most of your editing in the Word document, but always, and I mean always, print a copy to read through at least once, if not more, to see the written work on paper. You will catch more on the printed page than you will on the computer.

Tuck yourself into a quiet room and read your work out loud. This will help you self-edit in all phases of your book. By the time my books are ready to go to press, I am beyond tired of my own writing. You need to read your book so many times that you don't ever want to read it again!

Writers Group

A good writers group can be a great resource for editing. There are all sorts of different arrangements that writers groups can be organized in. Time in between meetings can vary from weekly, biweekly or monthly. I don't recommend joining a writers group that meets less than once a month.

There are two general formats that writers groups often take. There are editing and constructive criticism groups and then there are support groups. When you are in an editing and constructive criticism group, you are expected to have a new piece of work or what you are reworking at each meeting. Often the group will either email out that week's work a few days prior or pass out the next week's work at the current meeting. This gives members of the group time to work on their own at editing and offering helpful feedback for what you are working on.

Each member of the group is expected to have new work for each meeting and to have spent time editing the other members' work prior to the meeting. With this type of group, you should expect each meeting to take no less than two hours and the group size should be no larger than 4 to 5 members.

If you belong to a writers support group, then what you get each week is support, ideas and shared knowledge about the industry. If you need help editing your work, this is a good place to single out a few people who would be willing and able to help you out. You can never learn too much or be too connected with other writers. There is great value in a support writers group.

Friends and Family

You might not have a family full of English teachers, but if you do, get them to help! Even friends and family members who aren't writers or editors can be extremely helpful. The more eyes that look at your work, the more likely that mistakes will be caught. Many friends and family actually belong to your target market, so their feedback is also priceless. It is better to get soft criticism from a friend or family member versus being slammed in a review on your published work.

You might luck out and get heavy editing from someone you never expected to add such value to your work. You simply do not know the talents of those around you.

Industry Experts and Peer Review

I got some amazing feedback on my book *The Art, Science and Business of Aromatherapy* by sending out early copies to people I respected in the aromatherapy industry. The input they shared with me really changed my book for the better. The value of peer review is priceless. Don't be afraid to ask authors and other experts in the category you are writing, to lend you their professional opinion.

Amateur or Professional Editors

Social media is a great resource to find referrals. You can also email other authors to see if their editors can assist you. Having as many eyes, especially well trained eyes, on your book before you publish is the best way to go. Even after you have editing done via crowdsourcing, friends and family, industry experts, peer review, your writers group and editors, you can still expect to have someone point out an overlooked error after publication.

The wonderful thing about CreateSpace is that even after you publish, you can go back in and correct any errors for free, before future printings. Simply put the email address you would like errors reported to in the front of your book; future errors will land in your inbox so you can take care of them.

I had one poem in my poetry book, *When I was Young I Flew the Sun Like a Kite,* which was written 25 years ago in a college advanced poetry writing course. It got reviewed by the teacher, my fellow poets, and was read by countless people over the years. It was reviewed by me when I added it to my book and again by my editor. It wasn't until a few months after publication that I realized the poem ended by saying, "Mr. Freud" instead of "Dr. Freud." *How did we all overlook that?* I simply went back through the whole book again and found a few minor corrections before uploading the new document into CreateSpace and Kindle.

CHAPTER 8

Formatting, Layout & Other Details

Page Layout

You have the option of formatting your own book in Word or if you own InDesign, you can use it. CreateSpace also has the options of downloading a blank Word template or a formatted Word template. Before you download the template make sure that you first choose the trim size. The default setting on CreateSpace is 6" x 9," which is what I chose for this book and for my poetry book *When I was Young I Flew the Sun Like a Kite*. You can click on the button that says "choose a different size" to see all of the options.

When you choose the blank template from CreateSpace, the Word document already has the correct margins for the size of your book. It does not contain a sample layout or page numbers. If you choose the CreateSpace Formatted Template it will contain a sample layout, page numbers that start in chapter 1 and sample headers. You can either start writing your book in one of these two templates or cut and paste your book into one of them.

For this book, I used the CreateSpace Formatted Template and simply cut and pasted each segment of the book into the sample areas that say, "Insert chapter _ here" depending on which part of the book you are working on. Technology gives me a headache sometimes, so if there is a simple shortcut or way to do it on my own, then I'm going to take it.

Build a Skeleton to Write Your Book

I start every book out with a skeleton that I fill out as I go. I find that if I don't know where I plan on going with my book, I can wander aimlessly down a number of rabbit trails. It helps me immensely to have a loosely defined plan on paper as I work.

The framework for my skeleton varies slightly from book to book, but the general framework I fill out starts in a Word document and includes prompts for working title, working subtitle, author name, publisher logo, front matter, a full table of contents, back matter, dedication and so forth. If you look at this book, you will see the finished version of these prompts.

Multi-tasking to fill in the Skeleton

When I am not working on writing, I work on some of the other details like getting my ISBN number, researching editors and/or cover designers. As an entrepreneurial author, you will have all the balls in the air. You will be the one solely responsible for the content of your book, the layout, cover design, promotions and so forth.

Having the skeleton layout helps to prompt the author what steps are left in the writing, layout and details of finishing the interior of the book. It isn't necessary to follow my recommendation for a skeleton to succeed. I am simply including this information as one direction that works for me as a guide so that you can find what works best for you.

You can hire people to help you out along the way with bits and pieces, but at the end, you are the one responsible for making sure it all comes together. The skeleton helps you remember the necessary steps along the way. I highlight everything that isn't set in stone yet to remind myself to decide on things like the book title, chapter titles and so forth. I use different colors to highlight the chapters I haven't yet written. Then, I work on the document until all the highlights are gone!

You can go to *Chicago Manual of Style Online* to find the most current edition of The Parts of a Published Work, which will give you every detail you need to design your book front matter.

Details, Details

Go over every detail of your book. I submitted my first three books to the Writer's Digest Annual Self-Published Book Awards in 2012. The only negative feedback and points taken off by the judges were for the details of the book layout.

It is the little things that a trained eye will be able to point out that are tell-tale signs of a self-published book.

Headers and Footers

The Headers and Footers are the main reason I choose to use the CreateSpace Formatted Template. Your page numbers must start as page one on the Chapter 1 page in the Footer. In Word to make page one start with Chapter 1, go to Page Number, click Format Page Numbers to open the Page Number Format dialog box. To start numbering with 1, click Start at, and type the number 1.

The Header section of the book, Chapter 1 should have the book title on the one page and the authors name on the mirrored page. Headers and footers are ready and waiting for you to fill out in the CreateSpace Formatted Template. Most books put the author name on the even-numbered pages and the book title on the odd-numbered pages.

Font

You should use a font that isn't one you use every day on your computer as a glorified typewriter. You should choose a font that is easy to read but slightly different than the default fonts in Word like Times New Roman and Arial. The default setting in the CreateSpace Formatted Template is Garamond. You want reading to be easy on the eyes so don't pick something off the wall. The font size should be somewhere in the neighborhood of 10 to 12 depending on your font. The default on CreateSpace formatted template is 11.

Justify

Every paragraph should be justified. Do not use align left or center. As you do your layout, you will need to keep an eye on what happens to the last sentence of each paragraph. If you cut and paste into your document, you can find a four word sentence spread out all the way across the page as Word attempts to justify the line. When you see this, it is easy to fix. Simply put your cursor at the end of that sentence and hit "enter." This will cause the last sentence to behave and get into line.

Spaces

Spaces give me heartburn. If you are like me and you took typing class in the 1980's or earlier, then you have the same ingrained habit I have when it comes to overusing the space bar after periods. The old school method was to hit the spacebar twice after every single period. Well, just to mess with us old school folks and with the advancement of technology, the new rule is to only leave one space between sentences. I don't even think about the keyboard while I type, so breaking the habit of double clicking the space bar has been a challenge for me. Two spaces is literally a typing crime these days.

To fix double spaces go to "replace" or use Control H. A pop-up window will appear. In the space for, "find" you are literally going to type a period and hit the space bar 2 times. In the space for, "replace" type in a period and hit the space bar 1 time. This will find all of your dreaded double spaces and wipe them away. Make sure you double check this after all the editing and changes are done on your document. Repeat the same process for various alternate sentence endings such as question marks, exclamation marks, quote marks and so forth.

Confession time: I just followed the directions above and found 752 double spaces after sentences.

Pick a Style

When it is time to start the editing process chose one style of editing to use throughout your book. The most common styles are the Associated Press (AP), Chicago Manual of Style and the Oxford Manual of Style. Traditionally AP was used for newspapers and Chicago has been used for literature. But as media morph, these choices have become more debated. Some say AP is more used for appropriate for online writing, so perhaps if you plan to place some of your content online, AP may be best. A longer list of styles can be found in Appendix 1 Resources section of this book.

The most important thing you can do is to choose your style and be consistent throughout the same book, article, blog post, etc. Leave yourself a note to about which style you chose for editing in case you do an update of the book at a future date. Also, you may want to start to compile a style list for with common choices, like, do you use the serial comma or not, do you spell out numbers, etc. If you have a style preference, it will also be helpful to discuss with your style preferences with your editor.

Omitting Needless Words

The word *that* has fallen victim to excessive use and overzealous editing. Some editors will excessively chop the word *that* out of your manuscript in an effort to remove all needless words. Sometimes *that* is optional, but other times *that* is mandatory and other times *that* can make a nice bridge. For example, "She whispered she wanted another baby" or "She whispered that she wanted another baby." In this case it sounds better to include *that* in the sentence. Don't overreact to the desire to omit needless words by cutting so much that it interrupts the flow of your writing.

Em dash, en dash and hyphen

The em dash (—) is one of my favorite punctuation marks. The em dash can take the place of commas, parentheses or colons. It can be used in place of commas to enhance readability and emphasis of a sentence. You can use a pair of em dashes to replace a pair of parentheses. Using em dashes in place of parentheses draws attention to the content. To emphasize the conclusion of a sentence an em dash can be used in place of a colon. There should be no spaces on either side of the em dash, however most newspapers set the em dash off with a single space on each side.

In most cases you can enter an em dash by typing a pair of hyphens between the two words you want to connect, and Word will turn the hyphens into an em dash. If this method doesn't work, you can also press [Ctrl]+[Alt]+- using the minus sign (-) on the numeric keypad on a PC. Another alternative is to hold down the [Alt] key and type 0151 on the numeric keypad. Or you can choose Symbol from the Insert menu, click the Special Characters tab, highlight the em dash and click Insert. If you are using an Apple computer you can get an em dash by using [Option] + [Shift] and [-] using the hyphen key.

The en dash (–) is slightly shorter than the em dash. The en dash is read as "to" or "through." It is used to represent a span or range of numbers, dates or time. There should be no space on either side of an en dash. On a PC press [Ctrl]+[Alt]+- using the minus sign on the numeric keypad. If you are using an Apple computer you can get an en dash by using [Option] and [-].

A hyphen (-) even narrower than the em dash and the en dash. The hyphen is used for compound terms. It should never be used in place of an en dash or an em dash.

Chapter Headings

Depending on the genre of your book, you may want to start all new chapters on the right side of a fresh page. All chapter headings generally take up the first half of the page and the new chapter starts on the lower half of the page. You will see this is automatic on the CreateSpace formatted template. This can create blank pages in between chapters. When it does, make sure you remove the header and the footer from that page.

Starting a new chapter on the right page is not necessary for all genres. Since my early books were technical, how-to and craft books,

I adopted the style that is common in textbooks and cookbooks. Spend some time looking through your bookshelves and even head to the bookstore to see what is normal in your genre for all the layout details.

Line and Paragraph Spacing

The big key is to stay consistent with line and paragraph spacing. One of the tedious layout steps of my book *The Art, Science & Business of Aromatherapy* was going back through the entire text to find whether the spacing was consistent with paragraph headings and space between the lines.

For instance I could do this:

> **Topic A**
>
> Topic A is my favorite topic.
>
> OR
>
> **Topic A**
Topic A is my favorite topic.

Both are correct, but if you are inconsistent with your formatting people will notice.

Paragraphs

If you are a blogger, there is a good chance that you are in the habit of writing short paragraphs with double spaces in between them. It is also probable that you've gotten out of the habit of indenting your paragraphs. For printed books, you should not indent the first paragraph on a page or the first sentence after a heading. You should indent all of the other paragraphs.

As I write my books, I don't worry about this detail because paragraphs will shift around during the editing phase. Once the editing phase is over, it is time to get serious about how your paragraphs appear on the finished document. Careful editing will eliminate extra space in your book and help shorten your page count. Extra pages equal extra costs.

Headliners and Capitalization

I have to slap my own hand sometimes on this one. I spoke and studied the German language extensively growing up. I picked up the habit of capitalizing ALL nouns. This habit spilled over into the English language, and I still catch myself reaching for that "caps" button even when I'm not writing a title or subtitle.

I have noticed that random capitalization has been running rampant lately. I'm not sure if it is phenomena of the texting generation or what, but you need to watch your caps. You should be using caps in titles, subtitles, first word of sentence, names of people or places, first word in a quote, a person's title like "Chairman," and a dozen other rules.

When in doubt you can check GrammarGirl.com or GrammarBook.com. If you prefer a book version look for *The Blue Book of Grammar and Punctuation* by Jane Straus or *Grammar Girl's, Quick and Dirty Tips for Better Writing* by Mignon Fogarty. Your editor should catch all of this, but it is helpful to keep your eye out for improper capitalization as you near your final draft.

In the title and subtitle of your book, you can go crazy reading all the different style guides. The general rule of thumb is you should capitalize the first word and last word, all the nouns, pronouns, verbs, adjectives and adverbs.

To Hyphenate or not to Hyphenate

This is another one of those ever changing slippery slopes. I like to hyphenate and sometimes I over use it. I've had two editors disagree on the subject. One of the big keys is to stay consistent.

The general rule of thumb for hyphens is to hyphenate compound words like absent-minded, U-turn or word-of-mouth when they are used as adjectives, adverbs or nouns. Hyphenate numbers when compound numbers are spelled out like twenty-five, forty-six and ninety-nine. And the good old fashion hyphen between syllables used to link a word when you run out space for the word on the line you are working on.

A hyphen may be used when not using one will cause confusion or odd spellings like semi-independent, or re-sign when you mean to be saying sign again and not resign. Again your editor should catch these things, but it helps to be aware.

Visually Speaking

Don't write super long paragraphs. Once upon a time, you had to wait until you finished your entire thought on a topic to change paragraphs. That doesn't work in today's rushed society. Readers look at a large paragraph and get visually overwhelmed. We have been fed small bites of information, headliners and paragraphs that are four to six sentences long.

Our society now requires more white space between sentences, hence the use of shorter paragraphs, the use of bullet points and numbered lists have become common. As much as you can, write like a newspaper reporter with short paragraphs and not like an old English author.

Look at every detail of your book once you have it formatted. Look for sentences or words that got deserted and left behind when the page changes. It is better to let a page end with an extra space than to leave a straggler behind. Overall, make sure your finished draft looks consistent.

Use Quotation Marks to Quote

I know that seems obvious, but I've seen my own writings about aromatherapy scattered all over the Internet. When you use another person's work word-for-word use quotation marks, cite the source and observe Creative Common rules, or ask for permission to quote the author. You can find the Creative Common rules at

Creativecommons.org.

Most authors print their policy and method for requesting permission to reprint portions or quote from their book in the front matter of their books. If an email address is not provided in the book go to the author's website to find contact information. In my book, *The Art, Science and Business of Aromatherapy* I requested permission from authors, large privately held organizations and guilds to reprint codes of ethics, standards and practices from their websites. Gaining permission was a very simple process and well worth the effort to ensure that I observed copyright laws.

Index and Glossary

Indexing in the back of the book is only useful for the paperback version of your book. If your book is a reference book, educational or a resource book, you should consider including an index in the back. If your book needs a glossary, it should appear in the print and digital version. I normally have two highlighters in hand when I read the physical final draft of my book to highlight keywords that need to be indexed and/or added to the glossary. Once you are in the Word version of your finished and formatted book you can use the "find" function to account for all the pages containing your index words.

Copyright

From the U.S. Copyright office, here are the main points about copyrights that you need to know.

- "Copyright is a form of protection grounded in the U.S. Constitution and granted by law for original works of authorship fixed in a tangible medium of expression. Copyright covers both published and unpublished works."
- "Copyright, a form of intellectual property law, protects original works of authorship including literary, dramatic, musical, and artistic works, such as poetry, novels, movies, songs, computer software, and architecture. Copyright does not protect facts, ideas, systems, or methods of operation,

although it may protect the way these things are expressed."

- "Your work is under copyright protection the moment it is created and fixed in a tangible form that it is perceptible either directly or with the aid of a machine or device."
- "In general, registration is voluntary. Copyright exists from the moment the work is created. You will have to register, however, if you wish to bring a lawsuit for infringement of a U.S. work." U.S. Office of Copyright, FAQ, at Copyright.gov

In summary

- Your published AND unpublished works are automatically copyrighted.
- Copyright covers your intellectual property and authorship but does not protect ideas or facts.
- Your writing is copyrighted the moment you write it.
- You do not need to register your copyright but you are more than welcome to do so for a $35 dollar fee via online registration or $65 for a paper filing.

The benefits of registering are that the copyright becomes part of public record and you receive a certificate of registration. Registered copyrights may be eligible for statutory damages and attorney fees if you win a lawsuit. Most copyright infringements can be handled with a simple email or phone call because many cases are simply a lack of copyright knowledge or an honest mistake. In the case of dishonest people stealing your works, you need to consider whether you have the financial resources to go to court and if the payout is likely to be worth enough to spend your time and energy on.

A Word About Copyrights

In some cases, it can be very simple to gain permission to reprint copyrighted material for commercial purposes. Most authors have directions in the front matter of their book or on their website about how to gain permission to reprint.

A reprint may be completely free in some cases, as long as the author is cited. In other cases, there may be a small fee, a contract to sign and specific instructions. In the case of music lyrics, it just isn't worth the effort or costs. I've tried, even when I had the permission from the original author. The costs, contracts and long term royalties required by the music producer are simply too much.

Some material quotes are covered by Public Domain and others may fall under Fair Use laws. I am not a lawyer, so I am not going to get into the nitty-gritty details of these laws here. I have defined them in the glossary. You should always do your research on every quote before you use it.

In my book *360 Degrees of Grief,* I wanted to use one of my favorite William Stafford poems called *Circle of Breath.* I wrote to his son, who sent me to the publishing house and they gave me a few specific steps to gain permission. They gave me the specific citation required, sent me a contract with usage spelled out, asked for a small fee and for a copy of the published book to be sent to the William Stafford Archives at Watzek Library on the campus of Lewis & Clark College. I happily followed every step and his poem now appears in my book. As a William Stafford fan and a Lewis & Clark College Alumni, I am honored to have one of my books shelved in the William Stafford Archives.

On the other hand, I wanted to end a section of *360 Degrees of Grief* with the lyrics written by a songwriter who is a friend of mine. He gave me permission and his co-writer gave me permission, but the music producers sent me a long contract and an ASCAP payment plan that was out of the question.

In this book you will see several quotes from *Be the Monkey* by Barry Eisler and Joe Konrath. They gave their permission universally in the front matter of *Be the Monkey*, "Please feel free to repost all or any portion of this discussion with attribution and a link back to the authors."

CHAPTER 9

Cover Design

The digital age has completely changed the purpose and design of book covers. Your cover has to pop on a computer screen and on a bookshelf. In a single design your cover needs to look amazing at the size of postage stamp for online sales and in a full size book. This is as challenging as getting the same concept across in a 140-character tweet as you would with a full page article. This is where hiring an experienced graphic designer can be useful.

I've learned a lot along the way. I probably would have done some of my covers differently if I were planning them now. My favorite book cover is *When I was Young I Flew the Sun Like a Kite*, which was a painting that I purchased from artist Mark Lucero. When I bought it, I made sure he knew I was going to use it as the book cover of my poetry book so it wouldn't infringe on any copyrights. The book jacket looks great in the 6x9" cover and just as eye catching in the size of a postage stamp.

For my book *Puffy & Blue* I hired Shoot Y'all Photography to do a photo shoot for the cover. I picked my favorites and then crowdsourced opinions. The input from my Facebook committee was immensely helpful. Using photographs, art, drawings and creative graphics that can capture a reader's eye is vital.

Font

You do not have to use the same font on your cover or title page as you do in the body of your book. Use a font that looks great when it is big and bold. You can use the same font inside your book on your title page. The font on the cover of a book is bigger than you expect. Depending on the font you should be using between 60 and 100-point size font.

Colors

My mother was an artist. When she painted, her pallet was full of bright, bold colors that could intimidate other artists. Don't be afraid of color because your book will be showing up on a screen with a white background. You don't want your book to blend in.

Impression

Your book cover should tell a story. To be exact, it should tell the story of your book in an image. It should leave an impression with the viewer that tells them what genre this book belongs in and what it might be about. Don't have a Harlequin book cover for a serious piece of literature. Be sure to choose font, imagery and colors that match the story of your book.

Informative

The cover of the book should have the title, subtitle and author's name. The back cover should have a compelling headline, introductory blurb and/or a list of bulleted information about what the reader will gain from reading the book as well as any book endorsements. All back covers should contain the author's bio, the ISBN and barcode.

When bookstores thrived across America, consumers picked up your book on the shelf and read the front cover and back cover to form an opinion of the book. Today consumers are looking for reviews and endorsements of your book on the Internet.

What you shouldn't put on the back cover, front cover or anywhere on or in the book is a price. As a self-publisher you want to have the flexibility to change your price at any given time. You could change it for a special time frame, because the economy has tanked and consumers are spending less or because the hot new price point is now $4.97 instead of $4.99. Give yourself the flexibility of changing the price at any point in the future by not adding it to the covers of your book.

CHAPTER 10

Pricing to Sell

On average most unknown authors will easily sell a few hundred copies of their book. Many authors are making a living at writing, some are supplementing their income and others are wondering when they might sell one more copy. Of course, this variance is true for all entrepreneurs. Some are wildly successful, some are supplementing their income and others are languishing.

There are several key factors to being a successful author-preneur.

- Price
- Branding
- Social Media Influence
- Blogging
- Genre
- Appearance of Book Cover
- Engaging
- Sticky-ness
- Stick-to-it-ive-ness
- Having a Plan
- A Solid Product to Market (i.e. your book)

Price Point for Physical Books

Picking a price for your book is like a game of rock, paper, scissors. What generally wins is the lower price because it will increase your volume. Selling a higher volume of books at a lower price beats selling a few books at a high price every time. Other scenarios may work, but unless you're a household name, your best bet is to pick a lower price. If you are not a well-known author, people are not willing to risk letting go of a high sum of money, but they will impulse purchase your book at a lower price. Once they love your work, you have a loyal customer.

In paperback, the best price point is $9.99 or below. If your paperback is thick, you may not be able to hit the $9.99 price point because CreateSpace dictates the lowest price you can sell your book for based on page count. You can play with the price in the royalty calculator to determine how close you can be to pricing your book at $9.99 or below.

If you have written a monstrously large book, consider selling the full version and abridged versions that are much shorter. You might also want to release the book in volumes. My book *The Art, Science and Business of Aromatherapy* was too large to hit the $9.99 price point. I now have the book available in the larger business version, currently priced at $14.99, and a smaller abridged version is available and priced at $8.99. I simply removed all of the business information and created *The Art & Science of Aromatherapy*.

Originally, I wanted to put a higher price on my aromatherapy book because it had as much information or more than aromatherapy textbooks I had paid in excess of $150 each. I chose to sell it for a price point in the mid 20's, but I have since learned that lower prices are much better.

You can change your price on CreateSpace at any time. You can also upload a new cover or a new digital file of your book if you need to update, change or correct something. There is no charge from CreateSpace. If you make a significant change, I recommend getting a new proof, but if it is minor you may choose to accept the changes without a proof. You can re-issue, change the title and cover, produce a special edition or abridged edition of any of your books, but the new book would require a new ISBN.

Price Point for Digital Books

The magic price points on Kindle are between $0.99 and $4.99.

70% Royalty Requirements

- In the 70% model, your Kindle price must be 20% lower than any sales channel of your physical book or digital book in any other sales channel.
- Your list price must be between $2.99 and $9.99.
- In the 70% model, you pay a delivery charge depending on the megabytes (MB) of your file. In the US, they charge $0.15 for 1 megabyte.

35% Royalty Requirements

- No delivery charge.
- Your list price must be between

  $0.99 to $200 for ≤ 3MB
  $1.99 to $200.00 for ≥3MB≤10MB
  $2.99 to $200.00 for ≥10MB

Changes in Kindle Direct Publishing File

You can change your royalty rate, price or even upload an updated version of your book into KDP at any time. KDP always gives a warning that it could take up to 48 hours for your book to be available for sale again but in my experience it has always been on the same day. KDP does not charge for making changes.

Amazon Prime

While you are in KDP, you will be asked if you want to participate in KDP Select. This option is relatively new and enables authors and publishers to share in an annual fund, which at the time of this edition was $11 million. If you choose this option, then your book is required to give the Kindle store exclusive rights for 90 days. Your percentage of the shared fund is based on how often your book is borrowed from the Kindle Owners' Lending Library, which is exclusively available to Amazon Prime members who pay an annual fee for this benefit along with many others.

While your book is in this program, you cannot make it available for any other devices. Your Kindle version will be offered for the price you set for all other customers, but will be free to be borrowed for a 1-month period by Kindle Prime members. The benefit of this program is that if a prime member loves your book they will often go ahead and buy it later or recommend via word-of-mouth or leave a review. Currently, you also get 5 days' worth of free advertising for every 90 days in the program.

It is worth taking a moment to read through the fine print on KDP to make the right decision for your book. Once you join the program, the book will be exclusive to Kindle for 90 days. You can choose to have the 90 days automatically renew or not. This could be a great opportunity to take a "wait and see" approach with the exclusivity going to Kindle while you work on the promotional side of your business. This option also buys you 90 days to postpone working on formatting your book for other digital devices while you turn into a promotional machine.

CHAPTER 11

Business Tips for Author-preneurs

I've had countless people tell me that they want to write a book. I've been asked, "When is the best time to write book?" My answer is always the same, "Right now!" It does not matter what time of year it is, your season in life, the current state of the economy or who you are. The best time to write your book is when you begin thinking of writing that book!

Make a Mess

Don't keep getting ready to get ready to write. Get started! If you keep sharpening your pencils and filing papers in your files, then all you will have is an organized office. Too many would-be author-preneurs are stuck in the planning phase and need to just jump in. Yes, there is a place for planning, but eventually enough is enough. Don't get stuck in the analysis paralysis. Make a mess and clean it up later with a good editor.

Make a Good First Impression

First impressions will sell your book. Your book cover, website and social media outlets will be the first impression people have of you as an author, business and publishing house. Your book description and marketing will cause the customer to want to read reviews and take a closer look at your books or not. While you think the book itself is the most important part, in reality, you have to attract your readers first. You must have a good book to keep them coming back and in order to receive good reviews. Getting them to sample your work in the first place is all about the marketing.

Invest in a good first impression from your book cover, Amazon Author page, Internet site design, to your business cards. Don't skimp on the website or book cover. This industry is saturated with "the best thing since sliced bread" books, and the ones that get noticed are those that grab the attention of the consumer. If you need help, contact a graphic designer that has experience. Make sure you check out their portfolio, and if they don't have the type or quality of work you want for your products, don't hire them.

Empower and Enrich Your Consumer

Your readers are looking to be entertained, empowered or enriched by their encounter with your book. Be open, honest, transparent and above all generous with your readers.

Know Your Market

Often businesses waste time marketing their products to the wrong consumers. Know who your books will appeal to. Meet the needs of your consumer group, and your success will follow. Determining who your audience is; tweens (10 to 12 year olds), teens (13 to 19 year olds), women or men, will make selecting a relevant and enticing cover even easier. Keep your audience in mind as you are designing your website and your social media outlets as well.

Most importantly, be true to your market once you know who they are. Write your book, marketing materials and social media campaigns with your target audience in mind.

Keep your Goal in Sight

If you are becoming an author-preneur so that you can be home with your family, keep that in mind. Put photos of your kids and the vacation you want to take with them on your desk and refrigerator. Visual re-enforcement will help you through those long days and nights of solitude it takes to be a writer. There will be days, lots of them, where you wonder why in the world you are going to all this trouble. Just remember what motivates you during those times and the little things will fade.

Treat Your Business like a Business

You should start out with a plan to be successful and profitable. That means that you need to track your expenses and profits so that you can file a tax return at the end of the year. I keep a running Excel spreadsheet because not all expenses and income will come to you with a yearly report. When I'm writing I can be a disorganized mess, but I track my expenses and income consistently.

Follow the Leader

There are so many success stories in the book industry and there's plenty of room for many more. Don't see competition as a negative; see it as a positive because you can always learn from them. It also means that you are positioning yourself in a hot marketplace. Like never before, an author's ability to speak to consumers honestly and forthrightly will supersede those that only talk at their market without listening to their market.

Build a Foundation

Your foundation includes your platform, your books and all the details of being a business owner. You need to start a separate business bank account, consider incorporating, trademark the important stuff, buy website names and so forth. The list can be never ending.

In 2012, I spent more money on my business than I ever had before. It was the year that I incorporated, trademarked, published *When I was Young I Flew the Sun Like a Kite*, re-launched my author website KaylaFioravanti.com and launched my publishing house website Selah-Press.com. I worried and fretted about making a profit with all those big one-time expenses in one year. As it turned out, I still made a healthy profit because I was only spending money that was sitting in my business bank account. I never used credit or borrowed against future income.

In 2013, my expenses are sure to be significantly lower, but my income from the four books I have on the market will continue. The expenses of editing, cover design and ISBN have long ago been reimbursed by past books sales. Now everything those books bring in is gravy and I continue to build a wider foundation with more books. If you have more than one book in you, then keep writing. I believe everyone has more than one book of experience, knowledge and passion in them to share.

Crowdsource for Ideas

My Facebook committee has been incredibly helpful in helping choose book names, cover design and general encouragement. Use your social media contacts to help inspire you, find out what is sticky and make decisions. After all they are a great sampling of your book's audience.

Crowdsourcing is cheaper than designing studies, hiring participants or consultants. They are free and they also get excited about your upcoming book because they were with you the whole way.

Provide Variety

On Demand has gone wild. You can increase your income streams by creating other merchandizing using On Demand suppliers. You can create T-shirts that you don't even stock but you get a percentage of sales from. And T-shirts and other gimmicks are free word-of-mouth advertising for you. This is a new avenue for me too.

As I started talking about my future book *Gogo Naughty Paws,* I started getting questions about whether I would have T-shirts, coffee mugs and other *Gogo Naughty Paws* merchandizing. With On Demand options for all of these avenues my answer was, "Why not?"

It might not be the right time or the right book for additional merchandising, but keep it tucked away as an idea for the future.

Are you terrified yet?

The good news is that it is easy to sell what you know, what you are passionate about and what you believe in. If you've read this far, you must be serious. You've got this. Just be transparent, share your knowledge willingly, be active and be sincere.

Worried about the Economy?

The good news is that any bad economy means opportunity for entrepreneurs. And you, my friend, are now an entrepreneur or author-preneur.

Remember, whether you are already in business and just adding being an author to your repertoire or starting from scratch, it is critical that you allow yourself to blossom right where you are. Stop waiting for all of your ducks to be in a row. Maybe your ducks, like mine, don't fit together in a straight line. The reality is that tomorrow my ducks will scatter everywhere, but I've noticed that when I move they always follow me.

My metaphoric ducks don't follow me in an orderly fashion, but they will assemble loosely in a forward direction when I move forward. If I hang back, they hang back, and if I throw up my hands in the air and surrender, they scatter. So the very best thing that I have found is to move in a forward direction toward my goal and allow my frenzied ducks to follow suit. Trust me; your ducks will follow you too! Are you ready? Are you moving?

Speaking of ducks . . .

When my son Keegan was 2 years old, we spent Christmas in Germany visiting my parents. At the time, they were living in a very small village in Southern Germany that we affectionately called Yonder Village. The picturesque village provided an inspiring view from the front yard of my parent's home.

The year of our visit had been a particularly cold winter in Yonder Village. The hard winter was evident every time we passed by the ducks that lived in Yonder Village's pond. Every time we approached the pond, the ducks waddled over to greet us with loud complaints as only ducks can do.

Often times, we would set out for walks to enjoy the outdoors and the view as we took in the crisp fresh air. We all loved to feed the ducks along the way, but Keegan took particular joy in the task, so he became the official duck feeder. One afternoon Keegan lost his duck feeding joy. The following story is all true. No ducks or humans were injured during the events of this story.

It was a bit of a walk to the duck pond. This particular time we decided to push Keegan to the duck pond in his stroller. The ducks were exceptionally hungry that day and loudly waddled up to greet us. Keegan squealed with delight as the ducks surrounded his stroller and as they did, the volume of their hunger cries increased. Piece by piece Keegan threw out bits of bread. The ducks raced each other for every scrap. As the chaos of the ducks' hunger increased, Keegan sped up his bread throwing. The faster he threw out the bread the more excited the ducks became.

Eventually Keegan could not throw the food out fast enough for the ducks. Before we could step in to assist Keegan, the more aggressive ducks jumped up onto his lap in an attempt to take the bread directly from his hand. Keegan reacted quickly. He shoved every last morsel of bread that was in his little hands directly into his mouth! With all the bread gone, the ducks squawked and quacked. The frenzy continued, but Keegan was done feeding the ducks. Their response to what he was giving them frightened him. He stopped participating by hoarding what the ducks so desperately wanted. With mom and grandma along all ended well for the ducks and Keegan.

The image of Keegan shoving the bread into his mouth when the demand for what he had overwhelmed him is a perfect example of what many businesses do when the demand for their goods or time increases suddenly. Many times, we sabotage the growth of our own companies by reacting the same way that Keegan did that day.

Let me give you a few prime examples of unintentionally sabotaging your own business.

- Hoarding—When an author-preneur insists on keeping tight reigns on every detail of their business, they can end up strangling their potential. When you do this, you limit the growth of your company and reduce the number of people you can touch. Ultimately, if you can't delegate, you will cripple your business forever. This is why I use a virtual assistant, editors and graphic designers.

- Panicking—When a deadline approaches and the writer can't imagine how to meet it, they often unconsciously sabotage it. When the inevitable deadline approaches, don't allow panic to set in. You have a choice to quit, buckle down to get it done or adjust your deadline.

- Ostrich Maneuver—Putting your head in the sand. You might be a writer and not an editor, or maybe a teacher and not a graphic designer, or a great communicator but a terrible planner. Know your weaknesses and when you cross paths with one, get help from people who are experts in your areas of weakness.

- Sitting on the Bench—Refusing to participate in social media because you don't understand it or don't have time for it is like sitting on the sidelines. Make sure you get involved and are an active participant so your audience is aware you are open for business on Main Street America.

- Reactionary Responses—Don't allow a bad review, constructive criticism or any other negative response to get more attention than it deserves.

- Excuse Driven—Don't make, "I can't because" be your mantra. Instead say, "How can I?" and find a way.

- Turtle Approach—The phrases, "I'm waiting for the economy to improve," "I'm waiting until the kids are older," "I'm waiting until I have more money in my bank account," are the mantras of would-be author-preneurs who wait until it is too late.

Stop Waiting

Take control of your own economy and stop waiting. Make progressive steps forward despite the economy, stage of your life or time commitments. If you stand still, then your personal income is slipping backwards faster than you can afford. Delete the phrase "waiting for . . ." from your vocabulary, accept the economy and circumstances of today and move forward. Don't spend a single day waiting. Spend every day working towards your vision. It can be scary sometimes, I know! But never getting around to fulfilling your desire to write a book is even scarier!

Do What Makes Money First

Focus on the money making aspects of your business first. Don't get distracted doing busy work while setting aside the most important tasks of your day. It is easy to choose to do the easiest things first and then get around to the hard things later (if you have time left over). Often times, the hard things are the things that help you make money. Your daily to-do list should say, "First, do hard things; second, do the hard thing that makes money first." Get up and write first, then do all the rest of it. Make finishing your book your top priority.

Review Your Marketing

Take a close look at brand "You" to make sure you are sending the right message to your customers at the right time, and that your books match your message. Evaluate every dollar you spend against how many dollars they return. Cut the marketing that doesn't have a good return and focus on the marketing that does.

Use Technology to Make Decisions

Thorough and up-to-date research is just a few key strokes away for author-preneurs. It is important to seek advice, do research and read the most current information on technology. Don't be afraid of bucking the system of yesterday to try something new. I used a Google AdWords keyword search to decide on the name of this book. I'd already selected a few titles that I really liked, but when I plugged them into Google AdWords they proved to be poor book title choices. I settled on the title *How to Self-Publish: A Guide for Author-preneurs* based on my Google research.

Word or Phrase	Global Monthly Searches	Global Monthly Searches
How to	414,000,000	226,000,000
Guide	101,000,000	30,400,000
Guidebook	246,000	110,000
Self-Publishing	135,000	74,000
Self-Publish	110,000	60,500
How to Publish	1,500,000	550,000
How to Self-Publish	110,000	60,500

"If you always do what you've always done, you'll always get what you've always got."
Henry Ford

Most importantly

Above all, do not repeat the seven last words of a dying company, "I never did it like that before!" Don't stick to what you have historically done. Focus on new ways of doing business that can open doors and introduce a large group of new and loyal customers. Shamelessly advertise your business in traditional outlets and social media sites. Ask for business through newsletters, social media, blogs and up-selling. Don't be afraid to get creative in ways that are not part of the history of your business.

CHAPTER 12

119 Steps to On Demand Publication

Here are 119 steps you can check off on your way to getting your first book published with a platform in place. Remember to breathe as you go through the process.

Simultaneously

1. Set a deadline.
2. Write the skeleton of your book.
3. Create an account with CreateSpace.
4. Create a password sheet.
5. Create a new "folder" on your desktop where you will store all documents created for this book.
6. Decide what your brand "You" is about.
7. Research and choose a name for your publishing house.
8. Pick or create one up close, clear, asymmetrical photograph of your face to use.
9. Pick a blogging platform—I recommend WordPress.
10. Sign up for a Facebook page -not your personal one.
11. Sign up for Twitter.
12. Sign up for LinkedIn.
13. Sign up for Pinterest.
14. Sign up for Pheed.
15. Sign up for Google+.
16. Sign up for YouTube.
17. Sign up for Goodreads.
18. Join a writers group in your area or online.

19. Sign up for any other hot, relevant social media site.
20. Watch, stalk and lurk to watch how successful authors interact on social media.

Simultaneously

21. Start writing your book.
22. Send a copy of your book regularly to yourself, or back it up, or put it in Dropbox.
23. Create a bio to use on all social media that is likeable.
24. Build brand "You."
25. Design or have a website designed with blogging included.
26. Create your profile on Facebook page.
27. Create your profile on Twitter.
28. Create your profile on LinkedIn.
29. Create your profile and boards on Pinterest.
30. Create your profile on Pheed.
31. Create your profile on Google+.
32. Create your profile on YouTube.
33. Create your profile on Goodreads.
34. Create your profile on any new Social Media site.
35. Start a Newsletter and collect email addresses.
36. Become an Amazon Associate.

Simultaneously

37. Keep writing your book.
38. Start blogging.
39. Start getting active on your social media by interacting.
40. Spend some time on message boards in CreateSpace learning.
41. Read other experts' work in your field or similar books.
42. Actively participate in your writers group by offering your work for critique.
43. Start thinking of cover ideas but don't get stuck here.
44. Reset your deadline.

Simultaneously

45. Keep writing your book.
46. Start looking for editing options.
47. Ask for referrals for book cover design.
48. Keep up with blogging.
49. Stay engaged with social media by sharing your progress.
50. Resist temptation to go on a political tirade (or other hot topic) on social media platform.

Simultaneously

51. Finish writing.
52. Read your finished work in your head while making edits.

Simultaneously

53. Read a printed version of your finished work out loud while making edits on paper. Make sure you add page numbers before you print in case you drop your manuscript.

Simultaneously

54. Ask your writers group, friends and family to read a Word version with "track changes" on.
55. Absorb criticism without quitting.
56. Review suggested edits and revisions and make the ones that work for you.
57. Resist crying about constructive criticism on social media.

Simultaneously

58. Send your revised manuscript to your editor with "track changes" on in Word.
59. Start work on your book cover.
60. Keep blogging and engaging in social media.

Simultaneously

61. Go over changes from editor slowly and carefully.

62. Trust your editor but make the final call on what changes to accept.

Simultaneously

63. After taking a day break from your book, re-read it again.
64. Ask an advisor, peer or family member to proof read again.
65. If you used an amateur editor, use a second one.
66. Finalize cover design.

Getting Started in CreateSpace

67. You should already have an account at CreateSpace by now. Simply go to the member dashboard and click on "add new title."
68. Put in the title of your book.
69. Choose paperback, Audio CD, MP3, DVD or Video Download for the type of project you want to start.
70. Pause to dream a little bit about what you could do with the Audio CD, MP3, DVD or Video Download options available to you in CreateSpace.
71. Choose a setup process between "guided" and "expert." (Always pick guided because CreateSpace is constantly improving and you don't want to blow past a new important step)

Title Information Step by Step on CreateSpace

72. Fill in title.
73. Fill in subtitle.
74. Fill in primary author.
75. Add contributors such as cover design, co-author, artwork, editor and so forth.
76. If the book is part of a series (or will be) fill in series title and volume number.
77. Answer edition number, language and publication date.
78. Push "save & continue."

ISBN Step by Step on CreateSpace

79. Get ISBN from Bowker via CreateSpace or add your ISBN.
80. Spend time reading the information CreateSpace provides to understand your options. On your first time through the process, it doesn't hurt to spend the time clicking on the underscored information written in blue that will open up boxes that gives you further details. Sometimes it says "what's this" and other times it is simply the name of the topic written in blue and underlined that provides a hyperlink to further information.

Interior Step by Step on CreateSpace

81. Choose "interior type" (Black & White or Full Color).
82. Choose "paper color" (White or Cream).
83. Choose "trim size."
84. Download "Word Formatted" or "Blank Template."
85. Click on the option to estimate your book's manufacturing costs just to get an idea of costs. This information might make you decide to use a smaller or larger font.
86. Begin the layout process either with a CreateSpace template or a formatted Word document.
87. Choose the font, margins, chapter headings and so forth.
88. If you have trouble, hire someone at CreateSpace or a friend.
89. Upload your book file.
90. CreateSpace will take over to see if your margins or other common errors have occurred. You will get an email either approving interior or giving you a list of things that need to be fixed. Make any corrections that are necessary and upload your book again. Save the PDF document that CreateSpace creates of your approved book. You may need this when you go to publish on Kindle and other devices.

Exterior Step by Step on CreateSpace

91. Investigate cover paper options. CreateSpace now offers

glossy or matte covers. I published my first matte cover book, *Puffy & Blue: The Chronicles of Nine Lives Together*, in February 2015. I am totally sold on the look and feel of the matte finish. If you want to see what a matte cover looks like for yourself, order a matte cover sample from CreateSpace.

92. Add your cover to the spine dimensions and back cover in CreateSpace to build the outside cover of your book.
93. Choose "launch cover creator" if you are going to do it yourself. This step is when you could choose to have a professional finish the cover using CreateSpace or give the required dimensions of your cover, spine and back cover to your graphic designer.
94. Upload your finished Print-Ready PDF Cover that includes the spine, front and back covers in high resolution.
95. CreateSpace will take over to see if your spine and cover are correct. They will look to see if common errors have occurred. You will get an email either approving exterior or giving you a list of things that need to be fixed. Make any corrections that are necessary and upload your book cover again.
96. Save the PDF document that CreateSpace creates of your approved book cover. You may need this when you go to publish on Kindle and other devices.

Step by Step in CreateSpace

96. Follow the steps in Complete Setup.
97. CreateSpace will take your entire file and review it.
98. If you pass CreateSpace review you will get the opportunity to proof your book. First "Launch Interior Reviewer" and when you are satisfied, order a hard copy proof.
99. Absolutely, without a doubt, order a hard copy proof.
100. Once your proof arrives go over it inch by inch, word by word, cover to cover.
101. Ask a trusted friend, peer or advisor to do the same.

102. Make any corrections necessary following the above steps in both interior and exterior, step by step using CreateSpace.
103. If you had no corrections then approve your proof.
104. If you have minor corrections approve your virtual proof after CreateSpace accepts the changes. If the changes were major then order a new proof and repeat the review process.

Distribute Step by Step in CreateSpace

105. Choose the channels you want to distribute your book through via Amazon. I always pick all the channels available to me, including the expanded distribution for $25.00, which makes your book available to bookstores and online retailers. It is a one-time fee and it pays for itself within the first month.
106. Use the CreateSpace calculator to see what your list price will mean for you in royalty via different channels. Unless you are amazingly well known or your book is too large, you should pick a list price of $9.99 or below.
107. Add a short description of your book.
108. Choose one of the BISAC categories, which are the Book Industry Standards and Communications categories. These categories are used by the book-selling industry to group books by subject matter.
109. Add your author biography—remember you already wrote it for your social media and website.
110. Choose your book language and country of publication.
111. Pick 5 search keywords and input.
112. Follow the final directions regarding "contains adult language" and "large print."
113. Push "save and continue."
114. Create your Goodreads Author page and do a book give-away promotion.
115. Sign into your Amazon Associate page, put in your ISBN # to get an Amazon Associate link to your book so that you can

earn an extra 4% or more as you promote your book using that link.

116. Add your Amazon Associate link to your new book to your blog, website and social media.
117. Shout from the rooftops on your blog and social media about your new book.
118. On Twitter write a tweet to me that says something like this, "@KaylaFioravanti I followed your advice and just published my new book (include a link)" You can put your link on my author Facebook page too.
119. Put focused energy into the entrepreneur portion of being an author-preneur.

Update of Page Numbering in CreateSpace

Here is a quick how-to guide for authors using the CreateSpace template for self-publishing. I first ran into page number problems with my book *360 Degrees of Grief: Reflections of Hope*, published in February 2014. Thankfully, on the last night before my deadline at midnight, my friend Sue Nadel volunteered her husband Steve to help me out.

After all the hard work of laying out a book for Createspace in one of Createspaces' formatted Word documents, you might notice that problems occur with your page numbering. Don't panic. It happens sometimes. You don't have to scratch everything and start over. I had the exact same problem when I formatted *Puffy & Blue: The Chronicles of Nine Lives Together*, published in 2015. I followed these same steps again to fix the issue.

Easy Steps to Page Numbering

First—Make sure you have created a page break after every single section of your book. You need a break between front matter, another between dedication, another for the forward and so forth. You need it for every change. In Word 2010, go to Page Layout, put your curser at the end of the section before, click Breaks, chose Page in the drop down menu and now you have a break.

Second—Now that you have breaks set in your entire document go back to the top of your document. From here double click in the footer section. This will make the rest of your document look like a ghost and allow you to work solely in the footer. Go through your entire document, turning off *Same as Previous* in the Header Footer Toolbar at the start of every new section by clicking Link to Previous in your menu to turn it off.

Third—After you have gone through your entire document turning off the Link to Previous, you can fix any missed page numbers. Highlight the area where your page number should be, in the Header Footer Toolbar chose Page Number, and in the drop down menu chose Current Position and Plain Number.

When there are blank pages between chapters remove the header and footer. On the following blank page I left an unremoved header and footer as an example of a detail to catch while reviewing the final proof of your book.

CHAPTER 13
Kindle Direct Publishing

I read a lot. I do the majority of my reading on Kindle. Yes, I miss the feel of real books and understand all the reasons many readers don't make the change from paperback to Kindle. I was won over by the ease of reading from a lighted surface, the ability to highlight passages as I go and easily find it again with a quick search, and the lower prices of Kindle books versus paperback. For me, there is no going back.

The negative side is that there is a higher rate of typos and formatting problems in Kindle books. Something happens in translation from Word to MOBI (Kindle format) automatically. Numbers and symbols can get replaced or vanish. Paragraph indents go haywire. Bullet points turn into unorganized clumps of words. Spaces appear between paragraphs like giant gaping holes and countless other little details.

It is not only self-published authors with books on the market with these issues. The good news for authors is that if you have the original Word document of your Kindle book it is easy to fix the formatting. The bad news for authors is that it is time consuming and tedious, but it is worth taking the time before you publish to Kindle or even to reformat a book you have online.

Inconsistent and Excessive Indentations

When you are working in Word on your paperback, you get the perfect paragraph indentation when you hit tab. For Kindle this indentation is too large. You want to cut it in half. Unfortunately simply resenting the tab does not always work because you will find random paragraphs with excessive indents throughout your document once you view it on Kindle.

You will get the most consistent indents if you move the "first line indent" tab on your ruler. (There may be a correct technical term for this tool, but I figured this phrase was a better way to say what I meant than arrow-thingamajig.) I work chapter by chapter by highlighting the chapter and then resetting the "first line indent tab." Once you do that, go back through your chapter and double check all the first lines of your paragraphs. If one got missed, reset it individually.

Trust me, the indent will look too small on your Word document, but once you view it in Kindle you will see how clean it looks.

Bullet Points

Just don't do it! Bullet points do not translate to Kindle so if you paperback has them you will need to find an alternative method for formatting that section of your book. Unless you know how to write HTML code it just isn't worth the time to even try to get them to lineup.

Magical Typos

It is true. When a Word document converts to MOBI for Kindle, there are little elves inside that knock random symbols, numbers and letters around. I am sure of it! Do the Kindle review step over and over and over again until you find all the little moves, shifts and blurps that occur. And then don't worry about it if down the road a reviewer knocks you for having a typo. You can fix it quickly, reload, double check and within a matter of hours you are back online with a cleaner copy.

Typos happen to everyone! In fact I am reading a NY Times Bestseller right now and I found 2 typos on one page just last night. One was a formatting error when the quotation mark got separated from the text and the other was a misspelling.

Be considerate to authors and drop them a note if you find a typo. But please don't feel the need to blast them in a review for being human and for the little elves that knock things around in translation.

28 Steps to Kindle Direct Publishing

Now that your CreateSpace book is complete, you are ready to create a Kindle version of your book.

1. From CreateSpace, choose "Download Kindle-Ready Book Cover to my computer" and "Download this file to my computer" for the interior.
2. Use your Amazon Password or create an account to sign into KDP.
3. Add a title to your bookshelf.
4. Enter your book details, including book title, answer if it is a series or has an edition number.
5. Enter publisher information.
6. Enter the same description you used at CreateSpace for your book.
7. Add contributors including editors, graphic designer or co-authors as needed.
8. Choose language, publication date.
9. You can't use the same ISBN number for your print and digital book. You can choose not to have an ISBN or purchase a second number.
10. Verify your publishing rights.
11. Add 2 categories for your book.
12. Add up to 7 search keywords. Verify that they are well used search terms by using the GoogleAdwords key word tool.
13. Upload your book cover that you saved to your computer in step 1.
14. Choose to enable or not enable digital rights management

(DRM) which I talked about in Chapter 2.

15. Upload your book file that you saved to your computer in step 1.
16. KDP will take over and check your file. You may get a notice of a possible spelling error. Be sure to check any alerts that KDP sends to you.
17. Preview your book using the "online previewer." You can check it on various Kindle Devices by changing the device name at the top.
18. Look at every single page, take notes of major issues but be aware that there is not one single layout that will look the same on every single device.
19. You can open up your Kindle Ready document and make changes to make the layout as easy to read as possible. If you make changes simply repeat steps 16–18 until you are happy with the way your book looks on most Kindle devices.
20. Verify your publishing territories.
21. Choose to receive the 35% or 70% royalty.
22. Use the royalty calculator to play with different price points.
23. Choose international prices by checking the box to automatically set price based on US price.
24. Choose to allow or not allow Kindle Book Lending.
25. Click the box above "save and publish."
26. Push "save and publish."
27. Kindle will take over from here and tell you that it will take up to 12 hours to be available in Amazon Kindle Store.
28. Promote, promote and promote some more!

CHAPTER 14

You're Published, Now What?

Before 2009 you might have sheepishly admitted that you were self-published. Then, the unbelievable happened, and the mammoth publishing houses that acted as gatekeepers to the publishing industry were challenged by an unexpected change in the industry. Being a self-published author is now something to be proud of. You're an indie, artisan and homegrown business person now, in addition to being a writer.

In previous chapters, I gave you the task of simultaneously building your author website, faithfully blogging and interacting on social media. Now is the time to truly put those efforts to work for you.

Ask for Reviews

Get reviews for your book before it is available for sale. You can do this by asking the people in your sphere of influence to read a PDF version of your book prior to it coming to market. If you crowdsourced your editing, ask your editors for a review. Also ask your social media buddies.

Don't be afraid to ask industry experts who you are connected with. Ask other authors for their reviews of your book. Once you get those reviews, put them in your marketing materials and on your website. Ask your reviewers to put their reviews on Amazon when the book comes out and generally shout the reviews from the roof tops. Reviews are the best word-of-mouth advertising.

Note to the reader of *How to Self-Publish, A Guide for Author-*

preneurs, please do me the honor of leaving a review of this book on Amazon. Thank you!

Do Free Giveaways

You can use your website and Goodreads to do a variety of book giveaways. The bonus of book giveaways is that they often translate into book reviews. The added bonus is that you often get great word-of-mouth out of free giveaways as the winner celebrates their winnings on social media. That celebration gets people talking, asking questions and maybe heading over to your website. The expense of giveaways is the cost you pay for the book, plus shipping. It is difficult to calculate the costs of NOT doing giveaways.

Help a Reporter Out (HARO)

HARO is a resource for reporters. It takes a bit of time and energy on your part, but it is the least expensive method to getting your name, book and/or products mentioned in a newspaper or magazine article without hiring a PR firm. You can expect a phone call from HARO within hours to up-sell you into other paid goods and services. Listen to their sales call and determine if any of their current services are appealing to you.

When a reporter wants to write a story with expert opinions and information they will post their request on HARO. If you are an expert on the specific topic they have posted, you simply pitch the reporter with your expertise. The reporter may ask to interview you on the phone or send you written questions with a deadline.

Send Books to Conferences as Door Prizes

If your book covers a specific area of expertise, there is quite possibly a gathering or conference for that topic. For instance, this month I sent out three copies of my books as door prizes to The Alabama Soap and Candle Association Annual Meeting, the Tennessee Soap and Candle Gathering and the Lone Star Soap & Toiletries Soapmakers Seminar. In return I was given banners on their websites as a sponsor, and my books will get plenty of buzz in the door-prize drawing. I have the potential of exposing new customers to my books at the conference. The same principle can be applied to other topics and events.

Social Media

Do drawings for your books on social media. You can offer one entry to your drawing for a copy of your book if they use any form of social media to spread your message. Ask them to tag you in the share so that you can see it and add it to your drawing. This method is great to get people sharing. I've done it in the past for one month with weekly drawings. You could do it for one week with daily drawings or use whatever timing works for you.

Even without a reward, ask people to share your book release announcements. Ask your friends, family and social media friends with a personal note and a simple prepared message for them to post.

Local Events and Stores

Local stores love local authors. They love being able to say that this particular book on their shelf is from a local author. You are not limited to only bookstores when it comes to the local appeal. Look for Made in 'Your State' stores, coffee shops and independent store owners.

Inexpensive Brochures, Postcards and Business Cards

You can use Vista Print or a variety of other printers for inexpensive business cards, brochures, address labels, postcards, posters, car magnets, totes and pens. Choose a few inexpensive marketing gadgets that will serve as great handouts and fun marketing tools.

Offer to Speak for Free

Unless you are already well known as a speaker, the phone won't start ringing off the hook. Be willing to speak at conferences, schools, events, churches, community centers, retirement homes and so forth for free. Pick up the phone or make a social media connection with people that can open those doors for you and make the offer. Being told no doesn't hurt too much; especially the twentieth time, but yes feels mighty good every time. You won't get to the yes unless you risk the no.

Do Virtual Book Tours

Old fashioned book tours are a dying art. That is okay because we have a whole new virtual world available to use. You can do a virtual book tour by connecting with bloggers and asking them to allow you to guest post on their blog. What is in it for the blog host? They get a day off from blogging, you can offer them a free copy of your book, and generate new hits on their blog by promoting your book.

Podcasts and BlogTalk Radio

There are hundreds of indie radio shows available as podcasts and on BlogTalk Radio. Find the ones that fit your genre and offer to do a live interview with them. Not only does it get the word out to their listeners about your book, but you can use the interview file on your blog long term.

YouTube Virtual Reading

Use YouTube to do a virtual reading of your book just as you would if you were at a bookstore.

Keep Stocking Your Virtual Shelves

Once your first book is done, be careful not to rest on your laurels. If you want to be one of those successful author-preneurs who actually makes a living at writing as their full time job, you will need to continuously stock your virtual bookshelves with new material while promoting your current book. The flexibility of CreateSpace and Kindle has allowed many authors the ability to publish short stories.

Send out a Press Release

You should compose a press release to send out to local media, target newspapers, bloggers and/or use a distribution service. Press Release distribution services help spread your message to a larger audience. I have listed a few resources in Appendix 1.

Enter Writing Competitions

There are positive and negative facets of entering writing competitions. If you win, you will gain publicity, win cash prizes, get a free trip to a writing conference and find a few other doors opened along the way. The only downside is that you might lose, and depending on your fortitude, it just might crush you. You have to decide for yourself if you are willing to take that risk.

Many competitions include written feedback from the judges. This information can be priceless and can help you improve your book. Some competitions allow you to choose a very specific category, which increase your chances of placing. My book, *Puffy & Blue: The Chronicles of Nine Lives Together,* was the 2015 International Book Awards winner in the animal/pet narrative category. That is a very specific classification, which my book fit exactly within.

Many book competitions have a fee and specific deadline associated with entering. The deadline can be a great motivator to put you on course to finish your book in time to enter. I have been both a contestant and a judge in writing competitions. I find that the process is a win/win for everyone involved, but read all the small print, weigh the costs of the fee and make an educated decision that is best for your business. I have included an extensive list of writing competitions in the "Resources" list of this book.

Dream Job

Everyone has different goals when they write a book or start out in any business. You might just want to supplement your current income or have the opportunity to quit your day job.

My current publication plan is to write two to three profitable books to every one nonprofit book I have a passion for. That way I get to keep doing what I love while providing a regular income stream for my family. If I were relying on my poetry book to bring in regular income, I'd be out getting a second job. I have three profitable books on the market allowing me to indulge myself by writing a book that is purely about my passion for the way words sound when they bump up against each other.

I love being a full time author, in my case, being an author-preneur affords me a great deal of freedom to be a wife and mother above everything else. This is my dream job, and I'm finally doing it full time.

Now go write a book and join me on the virtual bookshelf!

ABOUT THE AUTHOR

Kayla Fioravanti is a wife, mother and award winning author. Kayla's easy-breezy explanations and instructions make her how-to books easy to digest and follow. Kayla's books *How to Make Melt & Pour Soap Base from Scratch*, *The Art, Science & Business of Aromatherapy* and *DIY Kitchen Chemistry* translate complex scientific information, formulas and procedures into everyday English.

Kayla's poetry book, *When I was Young I Flew the Sun Like a Kite* gives proof that the mind of a scientist can live concurrently with the heart of a poet. You can read Kayla's inspiring life story in *Puffy & Blue: The Chronicles of Nine Lives Together*. In 2011, the tragic death of her mom inspired her to be the managing editor, publisher and contributing author in *360 Degrees of Grief: Reflections of Hope.*

Kayla is happily married to her serial entrepreneur husband Dennis. They are the blessed parents of Keegan, Selah and Caiden. Kayla and her family live in Franklin, Tennessee.

Kayla's blogs can be found on KaylaFioravanti.com and her website is Selah-Press.com. Kayla has a long history of contributing articles to multiple magazines including *Dermascope, Les Nouvelles Esthetique, Global Cosmetic Industry (GCI) Magazine, New York Metro Parent*, and the *National Association of Holistic Aromatherapists*. Kayla has been featured and has given expert advice for hundreds of magazines including *Real Simple, Self Magazine, Prevention Magazine, Good Housekeeping, Home Business Magazine, Women Entrepreneur, Elle, Redbook, InStyle Magazine, Woman's World* and more. She wrote a chapter in the book *Millionaire Mom*, *The Art of Raising a Business and a*

Family at the Same Time by Joyce Bone.

Kayla's Twitter accounts are @KaylaFioravanti, @SelahPress and @GogoNaughtyPaws. She can also be found on her Facebook pages for Kayla Fioravanti, Selah Press and GogoNaughtyPaws.

APPENDIX 1

Resources

Affiliate Programs and Ad Revenue
Ad Brite—Adbrite.com
Amazon Associates—Associates.amazon.com
Buy Sell Ads—Buysellads.com
Café Press—Cafepress.com
Chitika—Chitika.com
Clickbank—Clickbank.com
Commission Junction—Commissionjunction.com
Double Click—Doubleclick.com
E-junkie—E-junkie.com
Google AdSense—Adsense.google.com
Kontera—Kontera.com
Linkshare—Linkshare.com
PayDotCom—Paydotcom.com
Zazzle—Zazzle.com

Author Platform Building
Selah Press—Selah-Press.com

Blog and Website Platforms
Blogger—Blogger.com
Typepad—Typepad.com
WordPress—Wordpress.com

Blog Directories
Blog Carnival—Blogcarnival.com
Blog Catalog—Blogcatalog.com
Blog Explosion—Blogexplosion.com
Blog Flux—Blogflux.com
Blog Hop—Bloghop.com
Blog Hub—Bloghub.com
Blogarama—Blogarama.com

Bloggapedia—Bloggapedia.com
Globe of Blogs—Globeofblogs.com
My Blog Log—Mybloglog.com
Networked Blogs—Networkedblogs.com
Technorati—Technorati.com

Book Promotion Sites
Addicted to eBooks—Addictedtoebooks.com
Author Marketing Club—Authormarketing.com
Books on the Knob—Blog.booksontheknob.org
Digital Book Today—Digitalbooktoday.com
eBook Habit—Ebookshabit.com
eReader News Today—Ereadernewstoday.com
Free Kindle Books & Tips—Fkbt.com/for-authors/
Free Books Daily—Freebooksdaily.com
GoodKindles—Goodkindles.net
GoodReads—Goodreads.com
Readers Favorite—Readersfavorite.com

Cover Art
Birdsong Creative—Birdsongcreative.com
Jeroen Ten Berge—Jeroentenberge.com
Lucky Bat Design—Luckybatbooks.com
Rebecca Byrd Bretz—Rebeccabyrdbretz.com

Crowdcontests
99 Designs—99designs.com
DesignCrowd—Designcrowd.com
crowdSpring—Crowdspring.com

Crowdsource Fundraising
Indiegogo—Indiegogo.com
Kickstarter—Kickstarter.com
Pubslush—Pubslush.com
Unbound—Unbound.co.uk

Crowdsourced Macrotasks
Elance—Elance.com
oDesk—Odesk.com

Sparked—Sparked.com
RadMatter—Radmatter.com
Fiverr—Fiverr.com

Crowdsourced Microtasks
Sparked—Sparked.com
Amazon Mechanical Turk—Mturk.com
Cloudfactory—Cloudfactory.com
InnoCentive—Innocentive.com
Samasource—Samasource.com
Galaxy Zoo—Galaxyzoo.com

Digital Book Conversion
Calibre—Calibre-ebook.com
Folium Book Studio—Foliumbookstudio.com
iBooks Author—Apple.com/ibooks-author
Jutoh—Jutoh.com
Mark's List—list@smashwords.com
Selah Press—Selah-Press.com
Smashwords—Smashwords.com

Digital Device Publishing
iBookstore—Itunesconnect.apple.com
Kindle—Kdp.amazon.com/self-publishing/signin
Kobo—Kobo.com/writinglife
Nook—Pubit.barnesandnoble.com

Domain Registrars
1 and 1—1and1.com
Domain.com—Domain.com
GoDaddy—Godaddy.com
Name—Name.com
NameCheap—Namecheap.com

Editing and Proofreading:
Co Writer Pro—Cowriterpro.com
Lucky Bat Books—Luckybatbooks.com
Ready to Publish—Readytopublish.blogspot.com
Scribendi—Scribendi.com

Selah Press—Selah-Press.com

Find Talent and Freelance Sites
99Designs—99designs.com
Amazon Mechanical Turk—Mturk.com/mturk/welcome
Craig's List—Craigslist.org
Edit911—Edit911.com
Elance—Elance.com
Guru—Guru.com
Kirkus—Kirkusreviews.com
Task Rabbit—Taskrabbit.com
Writer.ly—Writer.ly/home

Free Images
Can Stock Photo—Canstockphoto.com
Death to the Stock Photo—Deathtothestockphoto.com
Life of Pix—Lifeofpix.com
Pixabay—Pixabay.com
Morgue File—Morguefile.com
Wikimedia Commons—Commons.wikimedia.org/wiki/Main_Page
Photo Everywhere—Photoeverywhere.co.uk
Big Foto—Bigfoto.com
Fromoldbooks—Fromoldbooks.org
Animal Photos—Animalphotos.info/a
Creative Commons—Search.creativecommons.org
PicJumbo—Picjumbo.com
StockSnap—Stocksnap.com
Unsplash—Unsplash.com

Formatting
52 Novels—52novels.com
Birdsong Creative—Birdsongcreative.com
Lucky Bat Books—Luckybatbooks.com
Red Staple—Red-staple.com
Selah Press—Selah-Press.com

Google Tools
Google Adwords Keyword Tool—
Adwords.google.com/o/KeywordTool

Google Alerts—Google.com/alerts
Google Analytics—Analytics.google.com
Google Reader for RSS feeds—Google.com/reader
Google Trends—Trends.google.com

Graphic Design
Eco-Office Gals—Eco-officegals.com
Julie Bredesen—Juliebredesen.com
Logo Bench—Logobench.com
Rebecca Byrd Bretz—Rebeccabyrdbretz.com

Newsletter Platforms
AWeber—Aweber.com
Constant Contact—Constantcontact.com
Emma—Myemma.com
iContact—Icontact.com
MailChimp—Mailchimp.com

On Demand Publishers
Author House—Authorhouse.com
Blurb—Blurb.com
Bookbaby—Bookbaby.com
CreateSpace—Createspace.com
iUniverse—Iuniverse.com
Lulu—Lulu.com
O'Reilly Media—Oreilly.com
Outskirts Press—Outskirtspress.com
Virtual Bookworm—Virtualbookworm.com

Online Communities
CreateSpace Central—Createspace.com
Critique Circle—Critiquecircle.com
Critters Workshop—Critters.org
Figment—Figment.com
Goodreads—Goodreads.com
Review Fuse—Reviewfuse.com
Wattpad—Wattpad.com
WritersCafe.org—Writerscafe.org

Photo Editing
Canva—Canva.com
iPiccy—Ipiccy.com
PicMonkey—Picmonkey.com
Ribbet—Ribbet.com

Photography
Boulay Photography—Boulayphotography.com
Alexis Arnold Photography— Alexisarnoldphotography.com
Shoot Y'all Photography—Shootyallphotography.com

Press Release Distribution
PR Web—Prweb.com
Business Wire—Businesswire.com
PR Newswire—Prnewswire.com

Press Release Templates
SelfPub—Selfpub.info

Resources
Adobe InDesign—Adobe.com
Amazon Associate—Affiliate-program.amazon.com
Amazon Imprints—Amazon.com
Author Central on Amazon—Authorcentral.amazon.com
Autography—Autography.com
BlogTalk Radio—Blogtalkradio.com
Bowker—Bowker.com
Business Info Guide—Businessinfoguide.com
Dropbox—Dropbox.com
Espresso Book Machine—Ondemandbooks.com
FeedBurner for RSS feeds—Feedburner.com
Goodreads—Goodreads.com
HARO—Helpareporter.com
Hashtags.org—Hashtags.org
Independent Book Publishers Association—Ibpa-online.org
Kindle Direct—Kdp.amazon.com/self-publishing/signin
Peter Shankman—Shankman.com
Shelfari—Shelfari.com
Trademark Electronic Search System (TESS)—Tess2.uspto.gov

Twubs—Twubs.com
Vistaprint—Vistaprint.com

Reviews
Readers Favorite—Readersfavorite.com

Small Business Support and Coaching
High Wire in Heels—Highwireinheels.com
Indie Business Network—Indiebusinessnetwork.com
Lucky Break Consulting—Luckybreakconsulting.com
Selah Press—Selah-Press.com

Virtual Assistant
Assist University (virtual assistants)—Assistu.com
Eco-Office Gals—Eco-officegals.com
International Virtual Assistants Association—Ivaa.org

Web Design
Birdsong Creative Birdsong Creative—Birdsongcreative.com
Eco-Office Gals—Eco-officegals.com
Selah Press—Selah-Press.com

Web Hosting
Eco-Office Gals—Eco-officegals.com
GoDaddy—Godaddy.com
Host Gator—Hostgator.com
Network Solutions—Networksolutions.com

Writer Associations
Academy Of American Poets—Poets.org
American Christian Fiction Writers—ACFW.com
American Society Of Journalists And Authors (ASJA)—Asja.org
American Society of Composers, Authors and Publishers—Ascap.com
American Song Writers Association—Americansongwritersassociation.com
Asian American Journalists Association—Aaja.org
Association of Food Journalist—Afjonline.org
Association of Writers And Writing Programs—AWPwriter.org

Authors Guild—Authorsguild.org
BookWorks Self-Publishers Association—Bookworks.com
Cat Writers Association—Catwriters.com
Construction Writers Association—Constructionwriters.org
Dog Writers Association of America—Dogwriters.org
Education Writers Association—Ewa.org
Garden Writers Association—Gardenwriters.org
Fitness Writers Association—Fitnesswritersassociation.com
Florida Authors & Publishers Association—Floridapublishersassociation.com
Historical Novel Society—Historicalnovelsociety.org
International Association For Journal Writing—Iajw.org
International Women's Writing Guild—Iwwg.org
Military Writers Society Of America—Mwsadispatches.com
Mystery Writers Of America—Mysterywriters.org
National Association Of Independent Writers And Editors—Naiwe.com
National Association of Food Writers—Certifiedfoodwriters.org
National Association Of Memoir Writers—Namw.org
National Writers Association—Nationalwriters.com
Native American Journalists Association—Naja.com
Nonfiction Authors Association—NonfictionAuthorsAssociation.com
Novelists, Inc.—Ninc.com
Pacific Northwest Writers Association—Pnwa.org
PEN America Center—Pen.org
Pet Writers Central—Petwriterscentral.com
Poetry Society Of America—Poetrysociety.org
Romance Writers Of America—Rwa.org
Science Fiction and Fantasy Writers of America—Sfwa.org
Sisters In Crime—Sistersincrime.org
Small Publishers, Artists, And Writers Network—Spawn.org
Song Writers Guild of America—Songwritersguild.com
Society of Children's Book Writers And Illustrators—Scbwi.org
The Catholic Writers Guild—Catholicwritersguild.com
The National Writers Union—Nwu.org
Washington Romance Writers—Wrwdc.com
Western Writers Of America—Westernwriters.org
Women's Fiction Writers—Womenfictionwriters.org

Women's National Book Association—Wnba-books.org
Writers-Editors Network—Writerseditorsnetwork.com
Writers Guild Of America—Wga.org

Writing Competitions
Agnes Lynch Starrett Poetry Prize—Upress.pitt.edu
Amazon Breakthrough Novel Award—Amazon.com
American Book Awards—Bookspot.com
Amy Writing Awards—Worldmag.com/amyawards/
Anisfield-Wolf Book Awards—Anisfield-wolf.org
Axiom Business Book Awards—Axiomawards.com
Beverly Hills Book Awards—Beverlyhillsbookawards.com
Book Pipeline Awards—Bookpipeline.com
Book Works Awards—Bookworks.com
Brooklyn Non-Fiction & Fiction Prizes—Filmbrooklyn.org
Colorado Independent Book Awards—Cipacatalog.com
Digital Book Awards—Digitalbookworld.com/the-digitial-book-awards/
Drue Heinz Literature Prize—Upress.pitt.edu
eLit Awards—Elitawards.com
Eric Hoffer Award—Hofferaward.com
Ernest J. Gaines Award for Literary Excellence—Ernestjgainesaward.org
FAPA President's Award—Floridapublishersassociation.com/book-awards
Foreword Reviews Awards—Publishers.forewordreviews.com
Friends of America Writers Chicago Literature Award—awchicago.org/awards.php
Friends of American Writers Chicago Young People's Literature Awards—Fawchicago.org/juv_awards.php
Glenna Luschei Prize for African Poetry—Africanpoetrybf.unl.edu
Global Book Awards—Globalebookawards.com
Gray Wolf Press Nonfiction Prize—Graywolfpress.org/graywolf-press-nonfiction-prize
Green Book Festival—Greenbookfestival.com
Hektoen International—Hekint.org
Hollywood Book Festival—Hollywoodbookfestival.com
IBPA Benjamin Franklin Awards—Ibpabenjaminfranklinawards.com
Illumination Book Awards—Illuminationawards.com

Independent Publishers Book Awards—Independentpublisher.com
Indie Book Awards—Indiebookawards.com
Indie Reader Discovery Awards—
Indiereader.com/authorservices/indiereader-discovery-awards/
International Book Awards—Internationalbookawards.com
Independent Publisher Book Awards—Independentpublisher.com
James Laughlin Award—Poets.org/academy-american-poets/prizes/james-laughlin-award
John Gardner Fiction Book Award—Binghamton.edu
Kindle Book Awards—Thekindlebookreview.net
Living Now Book Awards—Livingnowawards.com
Marlene Awards—Wrwdc.com
Milt Kessler Poetry Book Awards—Binghamton.edu
Moonbeam Children's Book Awards—Moonbeamawards.com
Muse Medallion—Catwriters.com/wp_meow/contest/
National Award for Arts Writing—Artsclubofwashington.org
National Book Critics Awards—Bookcritics.org
National Indie Awards—Indieexcellence.com
Nautilus Book Awards—Nautilusbookawards.com
Nelson Algren Short Story Award—lgren.submittable.com/submit
New England Book Festival—Newenglandbookfestival.com
New Voices Award—Leeandlow.com/writers-illustrators/new-voices-award
New York Book Festival—Newyorkbookfestival.com
Next Generation Indie Book Awards—Indiebookawards.com
Paris Book Festival—Parisbookfestival.org
PEN/Faulkner Award—Penfaulkner.org
Readers Favorite Awards—Readersfavorite.com/annual-book-award-contest.htm
Real Simple's Life Lessons Essay Contest—Realsimple.com/work-life/life-strategies/inspiration-motivation/second-annual-life-lessons-essay-contest
San Francisco Book Festival—Sanfranciscobookfestival.com
Spark Creative Anthology—Sparkanthology.org
St. Francis College Literary Prize—Sfc.edu
St. Martin's Minotaur/Mystery Writers of America First Crime Novel Competition—Mysterywriters.org/about-mwa/st-martins/
Sarton Women's Literary Awards—
Storycircle.org/SartonLiteraryAward/

Stowe Prize—Harrietbeecherstowe.org
The Beach Book Festival—Beachbookfestival.com
The Brunel University African Poetry Prize—Africanpoetrybf.unl.edu
The Sillerman First Book Prize for African Poets—Africanpoetrybf.unl.edu
The Tufts Poetry Awards—Cgu.edu
Writer's Digest Self-Publishing Award—Writersdigest.com/competitions/writing-competitions
W.Y. Boyd Literary Award for Excellence in Military Fiction—Ala.org/awardsgrants/wy-boyd-literary-award-excellence-military-fiction
Unbound—Shelfmediagroup.com
Young Lions Fiction Award—Nypl.org

Writers Conferences
Nonfiction Writers Conference—Nonfictionwritersconference.com
Portals Writers Conference—Corban.edu
Writer's Digest Conference—Writersdigestconference.com

Writers Group
Camp NaNoWriMo—Campnanowrimo.org
NaNoWriMo—Nanowrimo.org
Writers Meetup—Writers.meetup.com

Social Media and Tools
Bitly—Bitly.com
Buffer—Bufferapp.com
Facebook—Facebook.com
Goodreads—Goodreads.com
Google+—Plus.google.com
Hashtags.org—Hashtags.org
Hibari—Hibariapp.com
Hootsuite—Hootsuite.com
Instagram—Instagram.com
LinkedIn—Linkedin.com
MySpace—Myspace.com
Ning—Ning.com
Periscope—Periscope.tv

Pheed—Pheed.com
Pinterest—Pinterest.com
SocialBro—Socialbro.com
TinyURL—Tinyurl.com
Tumblr—Tumblr.com
TweetDeck—Tweetdeck.com
Tweriod—Tweriod.com
Twitter Advertising—Advertising.twitter.com
Twitter—Twitter.com
Twubs—Twubs.com
Twuffer—Twuffer.com
YouTube—Youtube.com

Speaker Resources
American Seminar Leaders Association—Asla.com
American Society for Training & Development—Astd.org
Free newsletter for speakers—Speakernetnews.com
National Speakers' Association—Nsaspeaker.org
Toastmasters—Toastmasters.org

Style Guides
140 Characters: A Style Guide for the Short Form—140characters.com
AMA (American Medical Association) Manual of Style—Amamanualofstyle.com
Associated Press (AP) Stylebook—Apstylebook.com
Chicago Manual of Style (CMS)—Chicagomanualofstyle.org
Christian Writer's Manual of Style (CWMS)—Amazon.com
APA (American Psychological Association) Style—Apastyle.org
The Elements of Style—Amazon.com
Franklin Covey Style Guide for Business and Technical Communication—Amazon.com
The Global English Style Guide—Amazon.com
The Gregg Reference Manual—Gregg.com
The Hollywood Standard—Amazon.com
MLA (Modern Language Association) Style Manual and Guide to Scholarly Publishing—Mla.org
The PR Style Guide—Amazon.com
The New Oxford Manual of Style—Amazon.com

APPENDIX 2
Recommended Reading

Magazines & Websites
Barry Eisler, For Writers—Barryeisler.com/writers.php
BloggingPro—Bloggingpro.com
Blogtrepreneur.com—Blogtrepreneur.com
BlogNation—Blognation.com
BookTalk—Booktalk.com
Chicago Manual of Style Online—Chicagomanualofstyle.org
Christian Writers—Christianwriters.com
Copyyblogger.com—Copyblogger.com
Dailyblogtips.com—Dailyblogtips.com
Ereader News Today—Ereadernewstoday.com
Grammar Girl—Grammar.quickanddirtytips.com
Guy Kawaski—Guykawasaki.com
Indie Book Reviewer—Indiebookreviewer.wordpress.com
IndieBusiness.com—Indiebusinessblog.com
IndieReader.com—Indiereader.com
JA Konrath—Jakonrath.blogspot.com
JeffBullas.com—Jeffbullas.com
Kayla Fioravanti—KaylaFioravanti.com
Kindle Daily Nation—Kindlenationdaily.com
KindleBoards—Kboards.com
Lorelle.Wordpress.com—Lorelle.wordpress.com
MichaelHyatt.com—Michaelhyatt.com
Midwest Book Review—Midwestbookreview.com
MobileRead—Mobileread.com
NetGalley—Netgalley.com
Nothing Binding—Nothingbinding.com
Preditors and Editors—Pred-ed.com
Probloggger.com—Problogger.com
Publishers Weekly—Publishersweekly.com

Purdue Online Writing Lab—Owl.english.purdue.edu
QuickOnlineTips.com—Quickonlinetips.com
ReadWriteWeb.com—Readwrite.com
Selah-Press—SelahPress.com
The Rebelution—Therebelution.com
Websitesetupguide.com—Websitesetupguide.com
Writer's Beware—Sfwa.org/for-authors/writer-beware
Writer's Digest—Writersdigest.com

Books on Writing

- *APE: Author, Publisher, Entrepreneur-How to Publish a Book*, Guy Kawaskai and Shawn Welch
- *Be the Monkey* by Barry Eisler and Joe Konrath
- *Bird by Bird: Some Instructions on Writing and Life*, Anne Lamott
- *Dan Poynter's Self-Publishing Manual: How to Write, Print and Sell Your Own Book* (Volume 2), Dan Poynter
- *Grammar Girl's, Quick and Dirty Tips for Better Writing* by Mignon Fogarty
- *Lessons from a Lifetime of Writing: A Novelist Looks at His Craft*, David Morrell
- *Self-Editing for Fiction Writers; How to Edit Yourself into Print*, by Renni Browne and Dave King.
- *Stein on Writing: A Master Editor of Some of the Most Successful Writers of Our Century Shares His Craft Techniques and Strategies*, Sol Stein
- *Story: Substance, Structure, Style, and the Principles of Screenwriting*, Robert McKee
- *Storytelling in the New Hollywood: Understanding Classical Narrative Technique*, Kristen Thompson
- *The Art of Fiction*, by James Gardner
- *The Blue Book of Grammar and Punctuation* by Jane Straus
- *The Hollywood Standard: The Complete and Authoritative Guide to Script Format and Style*, Christopher Riley
- *The Screenwriter's Bible: A Complete Guide to Writing, Formatting, Editing, and Selling Your Script*, David Trottier

•

Glossary

Every effort was made to define most unfamiliar terms within the body of this book. The following terms could not easily be defined without interrupting the flow of the text. They have been provided here for your convenience.

(dot) doc—File extensions from Word documents from Microsoft 2000, 2002 or 2003. CreateSpace allows you to upload your work as a print-ready .pdf, .doc, .docx, or .rtf.

(dot) docx—File extensions from Word documents from Microsoft 2007 or 2010. CreateSpace allows you to upload your work as a print-ready .pdf, .doc, .docx, or .rtf.

(dot) rtf—A text file formate used by Microsoft products (rich text format) developed in 1987 for cross-platform interchange. CreateSpace allows you to upload your work as a print-ready .pdf, .doc, .docx, or .rtf.

(dot) pdf—A Portable Document Format that allows you to convert documents, forms, graphics and webpages invented by Adobe Systems used as an electronic document exchange.

à la carte—The ability to pick and choose which services you want to use, each service has a separate item on a menu.

App—Also known as application software designed to help perform specific tasks on a computer or mobile devicc.

Author Platform— An author platform is used to create visibility, authority, and reach to a target audience. All of the aspects of an author platform should direct your audience back to your branded website. A platform can include social media, email newsletter, a body of published work, speaking engagements, YouTube or podcasts, a tribe, membership in organizations, awards, recurring media appearances or interviews and a branded website.

Bandwidth—The amount of data that can be transmitted during a fixed amount of time.

Big 6 Publishers—The six largest publishing houses that control traditional publishing including; Hachette Book Group, Harper Collins, Macmillan, Penguin Group, Random House and Simon & Schuster.

BISAC Category—Stands for Book Industry Standards and Communications categories and are used by the book-selling industry to group books by subject matter.

Blogosphere—The buzz word that represents the blogging community on the Internet.

cPanel—Is a Unix (operating system) based web hosting control panel that provides interface and automation tools designed to simplify hosting a website.

CreateSpace-Assigned ISBN—A free ISBN number using the CreateSpace Independent Publishing Platform as the imprint.

Crowdsourcing—Having work done, information, ideas or funding via a crowd of people online.

Custom ISBN—The author or publisher choses the book's imprint of record and pays $10 to Bowkers through CreateSpace for ISBN number.

Custom Universal ISBN—Can be used with any publisher. The author or publisher choses the book's imprint of record and pays $99 to Bowkers through CreateSpace for ISBN number.

Disk space—The available space on a magnetic disk.

Domain Registrar—An organization that is accredited by the Internet Corporation for Assigned Names and Numbers (ICANN) who has the authority to register domain names.

Drop-ship—When goods are shipped from the manufacturer directly to a customer.

EPUB—Is a free and open eBook standard by the International Digital Publishing Forum. EPUB is short for Electronic Publication. EPUB is designed for reflowable content that can optimize text for a particular display devise.

Facebook committee—A term I made up to represent my community of friends on Facebook who give me advice and direction when I ask.

Fair Use—Under the doctrine of "fair use," the law allows the use of portions of copyrighted work without permission from the owner. Fair use is a defense to copyright infringement. In some cases unauthorized use of copyrighted material is excusable if it falls under the grey area of principle of fair use. Under the Copyright Act, the fair use of copyrighted material without permission is allowed when used for: criticism, comment, news reporting, scholarship and research, parody, and teaching. These uses do not grant the right to use the copyrighted work in its entirety. Fair Use is limited to quoting, excerpting, summarizing, and making educational copies of the material.

Front matter—The pages that precede the main text of a book which includes the title page, copyright and disclaimer page, table of contents and preface.

Ghostwriting—To write for someone else.

Google AdWords—An advertising program offered by Google, Inc.

Hashtags—Are used to engage in Twitter conversations, find relevant people to follow, gain valuable social media insight and participate in trends. A hashtag can be a word or phrase proceeded by # mark.

Keywords—A word or phrase used to help index content on Web pages for search engines.

Indie Mastermind Cruise—#IndieCruise is an annual Caribbean cruise for independent artisans and creative entrepreneurs, hosted by Donna Maria Coles Johnson, founder and CEO of Indie Business.

ISBN 10 and ISBN 13—In 2007 the International ISBN Agency changed ISBN format from 10 to 13 digits.

MOBI Files—A MOBI formatted document with the extension (dot) MOBI used by MobiPocket Reader.

Plug-in—A set of software components that add specific abilities to customize the function to a larger software application.

Proof—A trial printed version of your book to be checked and approved before publication.

Public Domain—A public domain work is a creative work that is not protected by copyright and which may be freely used by everyone. Works become public domain when the term of copyright for the work has expired; has been forfeited or are inapplicable.

Retweet—Is a method of engaging in social media in which you share someone else's tweet. Here is an example on my Twitter feed today from @Donnamaria, "Wisdom from my friend --> RT @KaylaFioravanti Are You Running the Right Race?

http://kaylafioravanti.com/are-you-running-the-right-race #goals #dreams"

Royalty—Compensation for the use or sale of copyrighted works as specified in a contract.

Scripts—A list of commands that contain instructions written in a scripting language to generate pages on the Internet that can be installed and managed.

SEO—Is short for Search Engine Optimization. It is a strategy used to increase the amount of visitors that visit you website by obtaining a high placement on search engines such as Google, Bing or Yahoo.

Stockholm syndrome—Refers to psychological symptoms that occur when a person or group of people are held hostage and form a paradoxical bond with their captor.

URL—A formatted text string used by Web browsers to indemnify the network resource on the internet.

Viral—The spread of information, links, photographs and videos from one person to another on the Internet.

Virtual assistant—An entrepreneur who provides contracted professional administration and technical services while operating outside of the client's office.

Widget—A generic term that allows the user to interface with an application and operating system.

www.webopedia.com, www.merriam-webster.com, www.techterms.com or www.medical dictionary.thefreedictionary.com used to confirm definitions.

References

Eisler, Barry and Joe Konrath. "Be the Monkey—Ebooks and Self-Publishing: A Dialog Between Authors Barry Eisler and Joe Konrath." Joe Konrath. March 18, 2011. Used with permission, "Please feel free to repost all or any portion of this discussion with attribution and a link back to the authors."

Smith, Craig. "How Many People Use the Top Social Media, Apps & Services." Digital Marketing Ramblings. March 15, 2013. http://expandedramblings.com/index.php/resource-how-many-people-use-the-top-social-media/

Urban Dictionary. "Urban Dictionary Define Authorpreneur." Urban Dictionary. March 15, 2013. http://www.urbandictionary.com/define.php?term=authorpreneur

U.S. Office of Copyright, "Frequently Asked Questions About Copyright." Copyright. March 16, 2013. http://www.copyright.gov/help/faq/

Acknowledgements

Over the years I've taken calls from friends, family and strangers who were all asking advice on how to self-publish a book. I am grateful that God put people in my life who nudged me to write this book to share what I've learned with a larger audience. I owe many thanks to David Sanford, Donna Maria Coles Johnson and La Shonda Tyree for the nudges that led to inspiration.

I am forever grateful to my team of crowdsourced editors who all poured hours of their time into this project. Their talent, insight and direction made this book what it is today. Thank you Elin Criswell, Duane Bigoni, Patricia Di Gasbarro, Holly Port, Mary Humphrey, Rose Cunfer, Shila Nirola Laing, Cheri Perry, Petra Monaco, Alyssa Middleton, Carrie Petersen, Leigh Cronin, Pat Dunn, Debbie Richards, Kismet Andrews, Teresa Buchmann, Starla Ledbetter, Ron Carlson, La Shonda Tyree, Melissa Rivera, Robin Parker Schmidt, Maria Gelnett, Alana Rivera, Matt and April Leffingwell, Kim Jones and a special thanks to Jennifer Smith for her expert technical editing. Thanks y'all!

In 2015, I received a firm nudge to update the information in the 1st edition of *How to Self-Publish* to produce this 2nd edition. I am incredibly grateful that Loral Robben Pepoon of cowriterpro.com was willing to come along side me to produce the book you are holding now.

Most importantly, I owe praises to my Lord Jesus for the gift of writing and above all for the certainty of His saving grace.

"Whatever you do, work at it with all your heart, as working for the Lord, not for human masters, since you know that you will receive an inheritance from the Lord as a reward. It is the Lord Christ you are serving." Colossians 3:23 NIV

45983266R00088

Made in the USA
Lexington, KY
18 October 2015